ANGELS UNVEILED

Journey through Divine Realms:
Revealing Secrets, Unleashing Miracles

Dr. R.D. Manning

Unless otherwise indicated,

All scripture quotations are taken from the King James Version of the Bible.

Angels Unveiled: Journey through Divine Realms: Revealing Secrets, Unleashing Miracles

ISBN: 979-8-9888050-0-7   *E-book* version

Copyright © 2023 by Dr. R.D. Manning

All rights reserved.

Published By: Interactive Faith Ministries

P.O. Box 1615

Williamston, N.C. 27892

U.S. A

Interactivefaith.org

You can't copy or share this publication without the publisher's written permission, except for small quotes in reviews or articles.

First Edition: 2023

Dedication

◆

To my beloved wife, Karmen,

In the tapestry of my life, you are the most exquisite thread—woven with love, grace, and unwavering support. This book is dedicated to you, my constant source of inspiration and strength.

Your love has been my guiding star, illuminating the darkest of nights and making every triumph sweeter. Your unwavering encouragement has been the wind beneath my wings, urging me to soar higher and never lose sight of the path that God has set before me.

With a heart full of gratitude and a soul brimming with love, I dedicate these words to you, Karmen. You have been my constant companion and love of my life on this journey, and your belief in me has propelled me forward, urging me to keep pressing on the assignment that God has given us together.

As we continue to walk hand in hand, may our love story be a testament to the boundless power of love and faith. Thank you for being by my side and the love that fills my heart.

With all my love,

R.D. Manning

"ANGLES UNVEILED:
Journey through Divine Realms"

Revealing Secrets, Unleashing Miracles

Table of Contents

Introduction	Angels Unveiled - Exploring the Mysteries of the Eternal	9
Chapter One	Revealing Secrets, Unleashing Miracles	13
Chapter Two	The Veil Lifted - Insights into Divine Realms	19
Chapter Three	Angels in the Old and New Testament - Divine Messengers in Our Lives	23
Chapter Four	Examining Angelic Visits and Interventions in the Old and New Testaments	29
Chapter Five	Angelic Involvement in Human Affairs	37
Chapter Six	How Angels Aid in Unveiling the Mysteries of God	43
Chapter Seven	Discerning the Signs of Angelic Presence	51

Chapter Eight	Guidelines for Interacting with Angels	57
Chapter Nine	Unveiling the Unfathomable Depths of God's Mysterious Realm	63
Chapter Ten	Cultivating a Lifestyle of Seeking God's Mysteries	69
Chapter Eleven	The Role of Angels in Eschatology	75
Chapter Twelve	Angelic Involvement in Judgment	81
Chapter Thirteen	Exploring Divine Realms of Angels	87
Chapter Fourteen	Maintaining a Balanced and Grounded Approach While Exploring Divine Realms	93
Chapter Fifteen	Connecting with Divine Guidance	99
Chapter Sixteen	The Art of Manifestation	105
Conclusion	Reflecting on the Journey of Unveiling the Divine	111

Introduction

Angels Unveiled -
Exploring the Mysteries of the Eternal

In the depths of our existence lies a dimension that transcends the tangible, a realm veiled from our everyday senses yet woven into the very fabric of our lives. It is a realm where heavenly beings, radiant and ethereal, move in graceful harmony—a realm inhabited by angels. These celestial messengers have fascinated and inspired humanity for centuries, captivating our imaginations, filling our scriptures, and stirring our souls with their divine presence. In "Angels Unveiled," we embark on a transcendent journey beyond the boundaries of the material world, a journey that leads us to uncover the profound significance and hidden secrets of these celestial beings.

To explore the enigmatic realm of angels is to step into a world where the supernatural meets the natural, where the ordinary encounters the extraordinary, and where the finite connects with the infinite. It is a journey that beckons us to lift the veil that separates the seen, from the unseen, to peer into the celestial timeline of existence, and to glimpse the heavenly hosts who dwell just beyond our perception.

In the pages of this book, I invite you to join me as we embark on an exploration that transcends the ordinary and delves deep into the mysteries of the ethereal. As we venture into the celestial realms, we will unearth the profound significance of angels and uncover the secrets they hold. Through the pages of scripture, primarily from the King James Version of the Bible, and through the lens of faith, we will illuminate the path before us and reveal the hidden truths that have stirred the hearts of believers for millennia.

In my unique writing style, I will guide you through the journey of "Angels Unveiled," helping you navigate the ethereal dimensions of these celestial beings. Together, we will uncover their roles as messengers, guardians, and guides, understanding how their presence can transform our lives. Through stories, reflections, and scriptural insights, we will shed light on the profound significance of these heavenly companions.

But as we embark on this spiritual expedition, let us tread carefully, for the realm of angels is both awe-inspiring and deeply mysterious. It is a realm where faith and wonder blend, where questions may outnumber answers, and where humility becomes our guide. Our journey is not one of mere curiosity or idle speculation but a pursuit of faith—a quest for a deeper connection with the divine and a more profound understanding of God's intricate design.

Throughout this book, we will strive for balance and reverence, always keeping our gaze fixed on the Creator, not merely His creations. Angels, though magnificent in their own right, are servants of the Almighty, and they point us toward Him. Our journey into the celestial realm is, at its core, a journey toward a more profound relationship with God, enriched by our growing understanding of His heavenly messengers.

As you read the pages that follow, I encourage you to approach this exploration with an open heart and a receptive spirit. As we unveil the secrets, significance, and sacredness of angels, may your faith be renewed, your hope kindled, and your connection with the divine deepened. Together, we will lift the veil that shrouds the celestial realm and step into the radiant presence of angels, ready to be guided, comforted, and inspired by their heavenly ministry.

In the forthcoming chapters, you may find not only knowledge but also a profound sense of wonder and awe. For in unveiling the mysteries of angels, we are drawn closer to the heart of the Divine, where the ethereal and the earthly intertwine in a harmonious dance, revealing the profound interconnectedness of all creation.

So, dear reader, let us embark on this journey with anticipation and reverence, for the realm of angels is vast and wondrous. In our quest to unveil the mysteries of the ethereal, we shall find not only knowledge but also a deeper understanding of our own place within the cosmic timeline. Together, let us take a step beyond the tangible world and enter the realm of angels, where the divine and the earthly converge, and where the secrets of existence are unveiled before our eager hearts and seeking souls.

Chapter One

Revealing Secrets, Unleashing Miracles

In the quiet of your heart, have you ever felt the brush of unseen wings, the whisper of a presence not quite earthly? Have you ever gazed at the starry night and wondered about the celestial beings that dwell beyond our sight, just beyond the veil of the tangible world? If you have, then you are not alone. Throughout history, humanity has been captivated by the thought of angels, those mysterious messengers of the divine, who move between the realms of heaven and earth, bearing secrets and miracles.

As we embark on this journey through "Angels Unveiled," it's essential to begin with a firm foundation of understanding and faith. We will delve into the depths of scripture, primarily from the King James Version of the Bible, to uncover the profound truths about angels and their role in our lives. But before we unveil the secrets, before we unleash the miracles, we must first recognize the significance of these celestial beings in our personal journey of faith.

Psalm 91:11-12 - For he shall give his angels charge over thee, to keep thee in all thy ways. They shall bear thee up in their hands, lest thou dash thy foot against a stone.

In this timeless passage from the Psalms, we catch a glimpse of the guardianship of angels. They are assigned to watch over us, to protect us in all our ways, to bear us up in their hands. Believer, the first revelation we uncover is the divine assignment of angels as protectors and guardians in our lives.

The meaning for us, dear reader, is that as we journey through life's terrain, we can take comfort in knowing that God has appointed angels to watch over us. Their presence offers us protection and reassurance, preventing us from stumbling in our walk of faith.

Hebrews 13:2 - Be not forgetful to entertain strangers: for thereby some have entertained angels unawares.

The writer of Hebrews reminds us of a remarkable truth—angels may walk among us incognito. They may appear as strangers, as ordinary individuals, and we may entertain them without recognizing their celestial nature. Believer, the second revelation we uncover is that angels may be closer than we think, their divine encounters concealed in everyday experiences.

The meaning for us is that we should approach every encounter with kindness and hospitality, for we never know when we may be entertaining angels. Our openness to others may lead us to divine appointments and encounters that bring blessings beyond measure.

Matthew 18:10 - Take heed that ye despise not one of these little ones; for I say unto you, That in heaven their angels do always behold the face of my Father which is in heaven.

In the Gospel of Matthew, Jesus imparts a solemn warning and a profound revelation. He speaks of the angels assigned to the little ones, emphasizing their constant connection to the Father in heaven. Believer, the third revelation we uncover is the intimate relationship between angels and God on our behalf.

The meaning for us is that we should never underestimate the importance of even the seemingly insignificant individuals in our lives. God's angels are always attentive, and our care for the "little ones" is observed by the heavenly host.

Luke 15:10 - Likewise, I say unto you, there is joy in the presence of the angels of God over one sinner that repenteth.

In the Gospel of Luke, Jesus reveals a scene in the heavenly realms—a moment of rejoicing among the angels over one sinner who repents. Believer, the fourth revelation we uncover is the angels' participation in the celebration of our repentance and return to God.

The meaning for us is that our repentance and return to God are not solitary acts. They are met with rejoicing in heaven, and the angels bear witness to our transformation. Our journey of faith is not one we undertake alone; it is a journey celebrated by the heavenly host.

2 Kings 6:15-17 - And when the servant of the man of God was risen early, and gone forth, behold, an host compassed the city both with horses and chariots. And his servant said unto him, Alas, my master! how shall we do? And he answered, Fear not: for they that be with us are more than they that be with them. And Elisha prayed, and said, Lord, I pray thee, open his eyes, that he may see. And the Lord opened the eyes of the young man; and he saw: and, behold, the mountain was full of horses and chariots of fire round about Elisha.

In this gripping account from the Old Testament, we witness the prophet Elisha and his servant surrounded by an enemy army. The servant despairs, but Elisha prays for his eyes to be opened, revealing a heavenly host of horses and chariots of fire. Believer, the fifth revelation we uncover is the powerful assistance of angels in times of trouble.

The meaning for us is that in moments of distress, when it seems as if we are outnumbered and surrounded, we can have confidence that the heavenly host is with us. We need only seek the Lord's perspective to see the divine reinforcements that surround us.

Acts 12:7 - And, behold, the angel of the Lord came upon him, and a light shined in the prison: and he smote Peter on the side, and raised him up, saying, Arise up quickly. And his chains fell off from his hands.

In the Book of Acts, we find the miraculous account of Peter's deliverance, from prison by an angel of the Lord. The angel brings light into the darkness of the prison, strikes Peter's side, and frees him from his chains. Believer, the sixth revelation we uncover is the angels' role in miraculous deliverance.

The meaning for us is that in times of bondage, darkness, or imprisonment, we can trust in the miraculous intervention of God's angels. They bring light into our darkest moments and release us from the chains that bind us.

Genesis 28:12 - And he dreamed, and behold a ladder set up on the earth, and the top of it reached to heaven: and behold the angels of God ascending and descending on it.

In the book of Genesis, we encounter Jacob's dream—a vision of a ladder reaching from earth to heaven with angels ascending and descending. Believer, the seventh revelation we uncover is the angels' connection between heaven and earth, serving as messengers and conduits of divine communication.

The meaning for us is that angels are divinely appointed messengers, conveying God's messages and guidance between heaven and earth. They bridge the gap between the human and the divine, bringing heavenly wisdom and revelation to our earthly lives.

As we conclude this first chapter, may these revelations about angels serve as a foundation for our journey together. These celestial beings are not distant or irrelevant to our lives; they are messengers, guardians, and companions on our spiritual path. Just as they have played pivotal roles in the lives of biblical figures, they stand ready to minister to us today.

In the chapters that follow, we will delve deeper into the mysteries of angels, exploring their roles, understanding their presence, and experiencing the miracles they can unleash in our lives. The journey ahead is one of faith, wonder, and transformation—a journey that will unveil the secrets of the ethereal and unleash the miracles that lie beyond the veil. So, dear reader, let us continue this exploration with hearts open to the divine mysteries and spirits hungry for the revelation of angels in our lives.

Chapter Two

The Veil Lifted - Insights into Divine Realms

In the quiet spaces of our souls, when we allow our hearts to open wide, we can catch glimpses of the sacred beyond the veil. There's an unseen realm, a celestial tapestry interwoven with the divine presence, and our quest is to unveil the mysteries of this realm. Together, we'll delve deeper into the ethereal world, drawing wisdom from the timeless words of the King James Version of the Bible.

Ephesians 6:12 - For we wrestle not against flesh and blood, but against principalities, against powers, against the rulers of the darkness of this world, against spiritual wickedness in high places.

These words from Ephesians beckon us to recognize the spiritual battle that rages beyond the scope of our physical senses. Our struggle, dear friends, is not confined to the visible realm; it extends into the divine realms where principalities and powers contend. It is in these unseen places that our faith is tested, our resolve is tried, and our hearts find their strength.

2 Corinthians 4:18 - While we look not at the things which are seen, but at the things which are not seen: for the things which are seen are temporal; but the things which are not seen are eternal.

This verse reminds us that the tangible world we perceive with our senses is but a fleeting moment in the grand scheme of eternity. The real substance of life resides in the unseen realms—the eternal truths that transcend time and space.

When we shift our gaze from the temporal to the eternal, we begin to grasp the profound reality that our lives are but a brief journey through this world, guided by the hand of the Divine. Our faith, our hope, our purpose—they all find their anchor in the unseen.

Colossians 1:16 - For by him were all things created, that are in heaven, and that are in earth, visible and invisible, whether they be thrones, or dominions, or principalities, or powers: all things were created by him, and for him.

In these words from Colossians, we gain insight into the comprehensive scope of God's creation. The visible and the invisible, the earthly and the heavenly, all were crafted by the hand of the Almighty. Every throne, every dominion, every principality, and every power finds its origin in the Creator.

As we contemplate the vastness of the divine realms, let us remember that all things were created for Him. Every angelic being, every spiritual entity, all exist to fulfill His divine purposes, and our lives are intricately woven into this fabric of creation.

Hebrews 1:1-2 - God, who at sundry times and in divers manners spake in time past unto the fathers by the prophets, hath in these last days spoken unto us by his Son, whom he hath appointed heir of all things, by whom also he made the worlds.

Here in Hebrews, we find a revelation of God's communication with humanity throughout the ages. He spoke to our forefathers through the prophets, and in these modern times, He has spoken to us through His Son, Jesus Christ. The very Word of God, the embodiment of divine truth, became flesh and dwelt among us.

In this revelation, we see the connection between the divine realms and our earthly existence. The bridge between heaven and earth is Jesus, who not only created the worlds but also reconciles us with the Divine. Through Him, we can partake in the mysteries of the unseen realms.

1 Corinthians 2:9 - But as it is written, Eye hath not seen, nor ear heard, neither have entered into the heart of man, the things which God hath prepared for them that love him.

In these words, we glimpse the unfathomable depths of God's love and the mysteries that await those who love Him. The human senses, limited as they are, cannot fully grasp the glorious treasures that God has prepared for His beloved.

It is in the unseen, the divine realms, that the true wonders of God's love are unveiled. As we deepen our understanding of these realms, we come to realize that our journey of faith is a thrilling exploration of the boundless love and grace of our Creator.

Dear friends, may we continue our journey with open hearts and a longing for the divine realms. As we explore the unseen, may our faith be strengthened, our hope renewed, and our souls enriched with the knowledge that we are partakers of the eternal mysteries of the Divine.

Chapter Three

◆

Angels in the Old and New Testament - Divine Messengers in Our Lives

In the sacred pages of the King James Version of the Bible, we embark on a journey that will deepen our understanding of angels and their significant role in the story of humanity. From the earliest chapters of Genesis to the climactic revelations in the New Testament, angels have been steadfast messengers of the Divine, guiding us, protecting us, and reminding us of God's boundless love. But it's not just ancient history; these angelic encounters hold profound meaning for our lives today. Let us delve into the scriptures and unearth the wisdom that lies within.

Genesis 16:7-8 - And the angel of the Lord found her by a fountain of water in the wilderness, by the fountain in the way to Shur. And he said, Hagar, Sarai's maid, whence camest thou? and whither wilt thou go? And she said, I flee from the face of my mistress Sarai.

Our journey begins in the book of Genesis, where we encounter Hagar, a woman cast into the wilderness. In her despair, she is visited by the angel of the Lord. This divine encounter reminds us that angels are not limited to heavenly proclamations; they also come to us in moments of distress and despair.

Beloved, when we find ourselves in the wilderness of life, feeling abandoned and alone, the angelic message is clear: God sees us, knows our pain, and is with us in our darkest moments. The wilderness becomes a place of revelation, where we encounter the comforting presence of angels.

Exodus 14:19 - And the angel of God, which went before the camp of Israel, removed and went behind them; and the pillar of the cloud went from before their face, and stood behind them.

As the Israelites fled from Egypt and found themselves trapped at the edge of the Red Sea, they were guided by a pillar of cloud and fire—a tangible manifestation of God's presence. But it was also an angel of God who went before them, leading the way.

This scripture teaches us that angels are not only messengers but also leaders and protectors. Just as the angel led the Israelites through the Red Sea to safety, we can trust that in our moments of uncertainty, angels guide our steps, ensuring we reach the promised land that God has prepared for us.

Judges 6:11-12 - And there came an angel of the Lord, and sat under an oak which was in Ophrah, that pertained unto Joash the Abiezrite: and his son Gideon threshed wheat by the winepress, to hide it from the Midianites. And the angel of the Lord appeared unto him, and said unto him, The Lord is with thee, thou mighty man of valour.

In the book of Judges, we meet Gideon, an unlikely hero who hides from the Midianites. In his moment of doubt and fear, an angel of the Lord appears and calls him a mighty man of valor. This encounter reveals the transformative power of angelic messages.

Dear believer, like Gideon, you may feel inadequate and afraid at times. But remember, when the angel of the Lord speaks, ordinary men and women become vessels of extraordinary courage and strength. The same angelic message holds true for you: "The Lord is with thee."

Luke 1:26-28 - And in the sixth month the angel Gabriel was sent from God unto a city of Galilee, named Nazareth, to a virgin espoused to a man whose name was Joseph, of the house of David; and the virgin's name was Mary. And the angel came in unto her, and said, Hail, thou that art highly favoured, the Lord is with thee: blessed art thou among women.

Turning to the New Testament, we encounter the angel Gabriel visiting the young Virgin Mary. The angel's proclamation carries a message of divine favor and blessing. Mary, chosen to bear the Son of God, receives a heavenly announcement that transforms her life forever.

Believer, in Mary's story, we see that angels bring messages of favor and blessing to those whom God has chosen for a special purpose. You, too, are highly favored in the eyes of the Lord, and angels continue to bring messages of divine favor into your life.

Matthew 2:13 - And when they were departed, behold, the angel of the Lord appeareth to Joseph in a dream, saying, Arise, and take the young child and his mother, and flee into Egypt, and be thou there until I bring thee word: for Herod will seek the young child to destroy him.

In the story of Jesus' birth, we witness another angelic intervention, this time in a dream to Joseph. The angel instructs him to flee to Egypt to protect the young child from King Herod's threat. This scripture demonstrates that angels guide us through the perils of life, ensuring our safety.

As believers, we can trust that angels continue to watch over us, providing guidance and protection when we face dangers or uncertainties. Their messages often come in the form of divine nudges, dreams, or intuitive promptings, guiding us toward the path of safety and God's purpose.

Acts 12:7 - And, behold, the angel of the Lord came upon him, and a light shined in the prison: and he smote Peter on the side, and raised him up, saying, Arise up quickly. And his chains fell off from his hands.

In the book of Acts, we witness the miraculous rescue of the apostle Peter from prison. An angel of the Lord appears, and in the midst of darkness and captivity, a radiant light shines, chains fall away, and Peter is set free.

This scripture serves as a powerful reminder that angels are agents of liberation. They break the chains that bind us, whether those chains are physical, emotional, or spiritual. When we find ourselves imprisoned by circumstances or fear, angels come to release us into the freedom and purpose God has for our lives.

Hebrews 13:2 - Be not forgetful to entertain strangers: for thereby some have entertained angels unawares.

The writer of Hebrews encourages us not to underestimate the significance of hospitality toward strangers, for in doing so, we may entertain angels without even realizing it.

Beloved, this verse reminds us that angelic encounters are not always grand and dramatic; sometimes, they come in the form of everyday interactions with those around us. When we extend kindness and love to others, we create opportunities for divine encounters that bless both the giver and the receiver.

Revelation 22:8-9 - And I John saw these things, and heard them. And when I had heard and seen, I fell down to worship before the feet of the angel which shewed me these things. Then saith he unto me, See thou do it not: for I am thy fellowservant, and of thy brethren the prophets, and of them which keep the sayings of this book: worship God.

In the closing pages of the Bible, the apostle John falls at the feet of an angel, overcome by the awe-inspiring visions he has witnessed. The angel's response is a profound revelation: he is not to be worshipped, for he is a fellow servant, one of the brethren of the prophets.

This scripture reminds us that angels, while majestic and powerful, are not objects of worship. Instead, they point us to the One who deserves all our adoration and praise—God Himself. Angels serve as messengers and guides, always directing our hearts toward the Divine.

Believer, as we explore these angelic encounters in the Old and New Testament, let us not view them merely as stories from the past. These encounters hold deep significance for our lives today. Just as Hagar found comfort in her wilderness, Gideon discovered his valor, and Mary received divine favor, we too can experience the presence and guidance of angels.

May we open our hearts to the possibility of angelic encounters in our daily lives. Let us heed the messages of guidance, favor, and protection that angels bring, and may our faith be strengthened as we recognize that we are not alone on this journey. Angels continue to be messengers of the Divine, guiding us toward the fulfillment of God's purpose and the realization of His boundless love.

Chapter Four

———•••⬦•••———

Examining Angelic Visits and Interventions in the Old and New Testaments

In the sacred pages of the King James Version of the Bible, we uncover a fabric woven with the threads of angelic encounters—divine visitations that span the ages. From the dawning of creation to the revelation of God's kingdom, angels have been God's messengers and ministers to humanity. As we explore these encounters, we shall not merely recount tales of antiquity but seek profound meaning and practical applications for the believer's life today.

Genesis 18:1-3 - And the Lord appeared unto him in the plains of Mamre: and he sat in the tent door in the heat of the day; And he lift up his eyes and looked, and, lo, three men stood by him: and when he saw them, he ran to meet them from the tent door, and bowed himself toward the ground, And said, My Lord, if now I have found favour in thy sight, pass not away, I pray thee, from thy servant.

Our journey begins with a visitation to Abraham under the oaks of Mamre. Though the text initially speaks of "three men," these were angels sent by the Lord. Here, we find Abraham extending hospitality, unaware that he entertained celestial beings.

Believer, the lesson is clear: by showing kindness to strangers, we may unknowingly entertain angels. In our daily interactions, let us be mindful of opportunities to extend love and grace, for in doing so, we may encounter the divine.

Genesis 22:11-12 - And the angel of the Lord called unto him out of heaven, and said, Abraham, Abraham: and he said, Here am I. And he said, Lay not thine hand upon the lad, neither do thou any thing unto him: for now I know that thou fearest God, seeing thou hast not withheld thy son, thine only son from me.

In the same narrative, the angel of the Lord intervenes as Abraham prepares to sacrifice his son, Isaac. The angel's message is clear: God acknowledges Abraham's faithfulness and obedience.

Believer, like Abraham, we encounter moments of testing and sacrifice. In these moments, remember that God sees your heart and knows your devotion. Just as the angel intervened for Abraham, God will provide a way when you trust in Him.

Genesis 28:12 - And he dreamed, and behold a ladder set up on the earth, and the top of it reached to heaven: and behold the angels of God ascending and descending on it.

Jacob's dream of a ladder extending from earth to heaven reveals a profound truth: angels serve as messengers and intermediaries between heaven and earth. They ascend to carry our petitions to God and descend with His blessings and guidance.

Believer, consider your prayers as incense ascending to the throne of God. Have confidence that angels are engaged in this sacred exchange, bringing answers, direction, and divine favor to your life.

Exodus 3:2-4 - And the angel of the Lord appeared unto him in a flame of fire out of the midst of a bush: and he looked, and, behold, the bush burned with fire, and the bush was not consumed. And Moses said, I will now turn aside, and see this great sight, why the bush is not burnt. And when the Lord saw that he turned aside to see, God called unto him out of the midst of the bush, and said, Moses, Moses. And he said, Here am I.

Moses encountered an angelic manifestation as a burning bush—a moment that led to his divine call and commission. The bush, though ablaze, was not consumed, symbolizing God's presence.

Believer, when you encounter the extraordinary in the midst of the ordinary, like Moses, pause and turn aside. God may be inviting you into a divine assignment. The presence of angels often heralds a significant moment in your journey.

Judges 6:11-12 - And there came an angel of the Lord, and sat under an oak which was in Ophrah, that pertained unto Joash the Abiezrite: and his son Gideon threshed wheat by the winepress, to hide it from the Midianites. And the angel of the Lord appeared unto him, and said unto him, The Lord is with thee, thou mighty man of valour.

Gideon, hiding from the oppression of the Midianites, received an angelic message that transformed his identity from a fearful man to a mighty man of valor.

Believer, even in your moments of fear and inadequacy, remember that God sees your potential. The angel's proclamation to Gideon applies to you as well: "The Lord is with thee." You are more courageous and capable than you realize.

Daniel 6:22 - My God hath sent his angel, and hath shut the lions' mouths, that they have not hurt me: forasmuch as before him innocency was found in me; and also before thee, O king, have I done no hurt.

In the midst of the lion's den, Daniel's faithfulness resulted in angelic intervention. God sent an angel to protect him, shutting the mouths of the hungry lions.

Believer, when you face trials or feel surrounded by danger, trust that God's angels are at work. Your innocence and faithfulness are noticed by the One who sends His messengers to shield you from harm.

Matthew 1:20-21 - But while he thought on these things, behold, the angel of the Lord appeared unto him in a dream, saying, Joseph, thou son of David, fear not to take unto thee Mary thy wife: for that which is conceived in her is of the Holy Ghost. And she shall bring forth a son, and thou shalt call his name Jesus: for he shall save his people from their sins.

Joseph, perplexed by Mary's pregnancy, received guidance from an angel in a dream. The angel revealed the divine origin of Mary's child and declared His mission to save humanity from sin.

Believer, in moments of confusion or uncertainty, be open to God's guidance through dreams and divine messages. Just as Joseph received clarity and direction, God desires to lead you in the way of righteousness.

Luke 2:9-11 - And, lo, the angel of the Lord came upon them, and the glory of the Lord shone round about them: and they were sore afraid. And the angel said unto them, Fear not: for, behold, I

bring you good tidings of great joy, which shall be to all people. For unto you is born this day in the city of David a Saviour, which is Christ the Lord.

The angelic proclamation to the shepherds in the fields near Bethlehem heralded the birth of Jesus Christ. Their message of good tidings and great joy reminds us that the Savior's arrival is a cause for celebration.

Believer, the birth of Jesus is not merely an ancient event but an ongoing source of joy and salvation. In times of darkness and fear, remember the angel's message: "Fear not," for the Christ child is still Emmanuel, God with us.

Acts 5:19-20 - But the angel of the Lord by night opened the prison doors, and brought them forth, and said, Go, stand and speak in the temple to the people all the words of this life.

The apostles, imprisoned for preaching the gospel, were freed by an angel of the Lord. The angel instructed them to continue sharing the message of eternal life.

Believer, when you face opposition or obstacles in your mission to proclaim the gospel, trust that God's angels can open doors that no one can shut. Their message to you echoes that of the apostles: "Go, stand and speak all the words of this life."

Hebrews 13:2 - Be not forgetful to entertain strangers: for thereby some have entertained angels unawares.

The writer of Hebrews reminds us of the importance of hospitality, for in doing so, we may entertain angels without realizing it.

Believer, extend kindness and hospitality to those around you, for in your interactions with strangers, you may encounter divine messengers. Angels often come in unexpected forms, and your generosity may lead to a significant divine encounter.

Revelation 22:8-9 - And I John saw these things, and heard them. And when I had heard and seen, I fell down to worship before the feet of the angel which shewed me these things. Then saith he unto me, See thou do it not: for I am thy fellowservant, and of thy brethren the prophets, and of them which keep the sayings of this book: worship God.

In the closing pages of the Bible, the apostle John encounters an angel who reveals visions of the future. John's instinct is to worship the angel, but the angel redirects his worship to God.

Believer, when you encounter the extraordinary, be cautious not to elevate messengers above the Creator. Angels, though mighty, are fellow servants. Direct your worship and adoration to God alone, recognizing that He is the source of all revelation and guidance.

As we examine these angelic visits and interventions in the Old and New Testaments, let us not view them as mere historical accounts. Instead, let us glean timeless truths and practical applications for our lives today:

1. Extend hospitality: Be open to divine encounters in your interactions with strangers, for you may entertain angels unawares.

2. Embrace moments of testing: Just as Abraham, Moses, and Gideon faced trials, remember that God sees your faithfulness and obedience, and He will provide a way.

3. Seek divine guidance: In times of confusion or uncertainty, be open to God's guidance through dreams and divine messages, as Joseph and Daniel experienced.

4. Proclaim the gospel: Like the apostles, be bold in sharing the message of eternal life, trusting that God's angels can open doors that no one can shut.

5. Worship God alone: Recognize that angels, though powerful messengers, are fellow servants. Direct your worship and adoration to the Creator, who is the source of all revelation and guidance.

Believer, the angelic encounters of old are not distant stories but living testimonies of God's involvement in the lives of His people. As you journey through life, be attentive to the whispers of angels, for they continue to deliver messages of hope, guidance, and divine intervention in the timeline of your own story.

Chapter Five

Angelic Involvement in Human Affairs

In the beautiful fabric of human history, there are threads woven by the hands of angels—celestial messengers whose presence and actions transcend the boundaries of the visible world. These divine beings have been God's emissaries, entrusted with significant roles in the affairs of humanity. As we embark on a journey to unveil the depths of angelic involvement in human affairs, we shall draw wisdom from the timeless words of the King James Version of the Bible. But this journey is not merely an exploration of ancient accounts; it is an invitation to consider the profound implications of angelic presence in our personal lives today.

Exodus 23:20 - Behold, I send an Angel before thee, to keep thee in the way, and to bring thee into the place which I have prepared.

Our journey begins in the book of Exodus, as the Israelites embark on their exodus from Egypt. God promises to send an Angel before them to guide, protect, and lead them to the Promised Land.

Believer, take heart, for you are not alone on your journey through the wilderness of life. God has assigned angels to keep you in the way, ensuring that you reach the place He has prepared for you. When faced with uncertainty, remember that your path is illuminated by divine guidance.

2 Kings 6:16-17 - And he answered, Fear not: for they that be with us are more than they that be with them. And Elisha prayed, and said, Lord, I pray thee, open his eyes, that he may see. And the Lord opened the eyes of the young man; and he saw: and, behold, the mountain was full of horses and chariots of fire round about Elisha.

Elisha and his servant found themselves surrounded by the enemy, but Elisha knew that angelic reinforcements were present. He prayed for his servant's eyes to be opened, revealing the chariots of fire and angelic host that encircled them.

Believer, in times of adversity or when you feel outnumbered, remember that those who are with you are more significant than those against you. Angels, like chariots of fire, are ready to defend and protect you. Seek the Lord's guidance to open your spiritual eyes and perceive their presence.

Psalm 91:11-12 - For he shall give his angels charge over thee, to keep thee in all thy ways. They shall bear thee up in their hands, lest thou dash thy foot against a stone.

The 91st Psalm provides a profound promise of angelic protection. God assigns angels to watch over us and safeguard our paths, ensuring that we do not stumble or fall.

Believer, take comfort in the knowledge that God's angels are charged with your protection. Even in the most treacherous terrain, they will bear you up in their hands, preventing harm from befalling you. Trust in their vigilant care as you navigate life's challenges.

Daniel 6:22 - My God hath sent his angel, and hath shut the lions' mouths, that they have not hurt me: forasmuch as before him innocency was found in me; and also before thee, O king, have I done no hurt.

In the midst of the lion's den, Daniel's unwavering faith resulted in angelic intervention. God sent His angel to close the mouths of the hungry lions, preserving Daniel's life.

Believer, when you face daunting circumstances or feel surrounded by threats, stand firm in your innocence and faithfulness before the Lord. Just as the angel intervened for Daniel, God's angels can protect you from harm. Trust in His deliverance.

Matthew 26:52-53 - Then said Jesus unto him, Put up again thy sword into his place: for all they that take the sword shall perish with the sword. Thinkest thou that I cannot now pray to my Father, and he shall presently give me more than twelve legions of angels?

In the Garden of Gethsemane, as Jesus faced betrayal and arrest, He declared His authority to call upon legions of angels for His defense. Yet, He chose to submit to God's will.

Believer, when you encounter injustice or persecution, remember that God's heavenly host is at your disposal. However, like Jesus, surrender your circumstances to the Father's will. He knows the best course of action, and His angels are always ready to fulfill His purpose in your life.

Acts 5:19-20 - But the angel of the Lord by night opened the prison doors, and brought them forth, and said, Go, stand and speak in the temple to the people all the words of this life.

The apostles, imprisoned for preaching the gospel, were miraculously freed by an angel of the Lord. The angel instructed them to continue boldly proclaiming the message of eternal life.

Believer, when you face opposition or obstacles in your mission to share the gospel, trust that God's angels can open doors of opportunity. Their message to you echoes that of the apostles: "Go, stand and speak all the words of this life." Do not be deterred by adversity, for divine intervention is at hand.

Hebrews 1:14 - Are they not all ministering spirits, sent forth to minister for them who shall be heirs of salvation?

The writer of Hebrews affirms that angels are ministering spirits, sent to serve and assist those who will inherit salvation.

Believer, recognize that angels are continually at work on your behalf. They minister to you in ways seen and unseen, guiding, protecting, and bringing comfort. Trust in their presence as you walk the path of salvation.

Revelation 1:1 - The revelation of Jesus Christ, which God gave unto him, to shew unto his servants things which must shortly come to pass; and he sent by his angel unto his servant John:

In the book of Revelation, we see an angel delivering the revelation of Jesus Christ to the apostle John. This divine message unveils the future and God's ultimate plan.

Believer, the same God who sent His angel to reveal His plan to John desires to reveal His purposes to you. Seek His guidance and revelation through prayer and study of His Word, for angels are involved in conveying God's divine messages.

As we examine angelic involvement in human affairs, let us internalize the following truths and apply them to our personal lives:

1. Divine guidance and protection: Like the Israelites, trust that God has assigned angels to guide, protect, and lead you on your journey through life.

2. Spiritual sight: Seek the Lord's guidance to open your spiritual eyes, enabling you to perceive the angelic host that surrounds you in times of need.

3. Angelic protection: Find comfort in knowing that angels are charged with your protection, preventing harm and ensuring your safety.

4. Trust in deliverance: In times of adversity, maintain your innocence and faithfulness before the Lord, trusting in His angels to deliver you from harm.

5. Surrender to God's will: Like Jesus, submit to the Father's will, even in the face of adversity, knowing that His angels are ready to fulfill His purpose in your life.

6. Proclaim the gospel boldly: Trust that God's angels can open doors of opportunity for you to share the message of eternal life, and do not be deterred by opposition.

7. Ministering spirits: Acknowledge that angels are continually at work on your behalf, serving, guiding, and comforting you as you walk the path of salvation.

8. Seek divine revelation: Just as John received divine messages through an angel, seek God's guidance and revelation in your own life through prayer and study of His Word.

Believer, the involvement of angels in human affairs is not a mere historical curiosity but a present reality. The same God who dispatched angels to guide, protect, and intervene in the lives of those who have gone before us continues to do so in our lives today. May you walk in the awareness of their presence, trusting in God's divine orchestration of your journey.

Chapter Six

◆

How Angels Aid in Unveiling the Mysteries of God

In the grand tapestry of God's divine plan, angels play a remarkable role as bearers of revelation and wisdom. They are the celestial messengers entrusted with unveiling the mysteries of God to humanity. As we explore the ways in which angels aid in revealing these sacred truths, we will draw upon the timeless words of the King James Version of the Bible. But this journey is not a mere intellectual pursuit; it is an invitation to apply these revelations to our personal lives and deepen our understanding of the mysteries of God.

Genesis 32:24-30 - And Jacob was left alone; and there wrestled a man with him until the breaking of the day. And when he saw that he prevailed not against him, he touched the hollow of his thigh; and the hollow of Jacob's thigh was out of joint, as he wrestled with him. And he said, Let me go, for the day breaketh. And he said, I will not let thee go, except thou bless me. And he said unto him,

What is thy name? And he said, Jacob. And he said, Thy name shall be called no more Jacob, but Israel: for as a prince hast thou power with God and with men, and hast prevailed. And Jacob asked him, and said, Tell me, I pray thee, thy name. And he said, Wherefore is it that thou dost ask after my name? And he blessed him there. And Jacob called the name of the place Peniel: for I have seen God face to face, and my life is preserved.

In this captivating encounter between Jacob and a mysterious man, we witness a profound revelation of God's character. Jacob wrestled with this man, and in the struggle, he sought a blessing. It was not until the breaking of day that Jacob realized he had wrestled with God Himself.

Believer, this account reminds us that God sometimes reveals Himself in unexpected ways. We may find ourselves wrestling with the mysteries of God, yearning for a blessing or a deeper understanding. Just as Jacob persevered, we too should persist in seeking God's revelation and blessing, even when it seems elusive.

Exodus 25:18-20 - And thou shalt make two cherubims of gold, of beaten work shalt thou make them, in the two ends of the mercy seat. And make one cherub on the one end, and the other cherub on the other end: even of the mercy seat shall ye make the cherubims on the two ends thereof. And the cherubims shall stretch forth their wings on high, covering the mercy seat with their wings, and their faces shall look one to another; toward the mercy seat shall the faces of the cherubims be.

In the instructions for the construction of the Ark of the Covenant, we encounter the imagery of cherubim. These angelic beings with outstretched wings faced each other, guarding the mercy seat—the place where God's presence dwelled.

Believer, the cherubim serve as a reminder that angels are intimately connected with God's presence and His mercy. Just as they guarded the mercy seat, angels continue to usher us into the presence of a merciful God. Approach His presence with reverence, knowing that angels accompany you on this sacred journey.

Numbers 22:22-31 - And God's anger was kindled because he went: and the angel of the Lord stood in the way for an adversary against him. Now he was riding upon his ass, and his two servants were with him. And the ass saw the angel of the Lord standing in the way, and his sword drawn in his hand: and the ass turned aside out of the way, and went into the field: and Balaam smote the ass, to turn her into the way. But the angel of the Lord stood in a path of the vineyards, a wall being on this side, and a wall on that side. And when the ass saw the angel of the Lord, she thrust herself unto the wall, and crushed Balaam's foot against the wall: and he smote her again. And the angel of the Lord went further, and stood in a narrow place, where was no way to turn either to the right hand or to the left. And when the ass saw the angel of the Lord, she fell down under Balaam: and Balaam's anger was kindled, and he smote the ass with a staff. And the Lord opened the mouth of the ass, and she said unto Balaam, What have I done unto thee, that thou hast smitten me these three times? And Balaam said unto the ass, Because thou hast mocked me: I would there were a sword in mine hand, for now would I kill thee. And the ass said unto Balaam, Am not I thine ass, upon which thou hast ridden ever since I was thine unto this day? was I ever wont to do so unto thee? and he said, Nay. Then the Lord opened the eyes of Balaam, and he saw the angel of

the Lord standing in the way, and his sword drawn in his hand: and he bowed down his head, and fell flat on his face.

In this unusual account, the angel of the Lord stands as an adversary against Balaam, who is on a journey with wrongful intentions. Balaam's donkey perceives the angel and refuses to move, leading to a series of events that ultimately reveal the angel's presence.

Believer, this narrative teaches us that angels can be sent as divine interceptors when we are headed down the wrong path. Even when we are oblivious to their presence, angels are watchful and ready to redirect us toward God's will. Be open to divine interventions that may seem unconventional, for they are often orchestrated by angels.

Daniel 9:20-23 - And whiles I was speaking, and praying, and confessing my sin and the sin of my people Israel, and presenting my supplication before the Lord my God for the holy mountain of my God; Yea, whiles I was speaking in prayer, even the man Gabriel, whom I had seen in the vision at the beginning, being caused to fly swiftly, touched me about the time of the evening oblation. And he informed me, and talked with me, and said, O Daniel, I am now come forth to give thee skill and understanding. At the beginning of thy supplications the commandment came forth, and I am come to show thee; for thou art greatly beloved: therefore understand the matter, and consider the vision.

In Daniel's prayer and confession, the angel Gabriel swiftly appears to provide understanding and insight. Gabriel's arrival is in response to Daniel's supplication, emphasizing God's favor upon Daniel.

Believer, when you seek understanding and revelation from God through prayer and supplication, know that angels are dispatched to provide insight and skill. Like Daniel, you are greatly beloved, and

God desires to grant you wisdom and understanding in the mysteries of His will.

Luke 1:26-31 - And in the sixth month the angel Gabriel was sent from God unto a city of Galilee, named Nazareth, To a virgin espoused to a man whose name was Joseph, of the house of David; and the virgin's name was Mary. And the angel came in unto her, and said, Hail, thou that art highly favoured, the Lord is with thee: blessed art thou among women. And when she saw him, she was troubled at his saying, and cast in her mind what manner of salutation this should be. And the angel said unto her, Fear not, Mary: for thou hast found favour with God. And, behold, thou shalt conceive in thy womb, and bring forth a son, and shalt call his name JESUS.

The angel, Gabriel's visitation to Mary is a pivotal moment in history. He announces God's favor upon Mary and delivers the message of the miraculous birth of Jesus, the Messiah.

Believer, the angelic announcement to Mary serves as a reminder that God's revelations can come in unexpected ways. When you find yourself in a troubling or perplexing situation, do not fear, for God's favor and His divine plan may be at work in your life.

Acts 27:23-24 - For there stood by me this night the angel of God, whose I am, and whom I serve, Saying, Fear not, Paul; thou must be brought before Caesar: and, lo, God hath given thee all them that sail with thee.

In the midst of a treacherous sea voyage, the apostle Paul receives a visitation from the angel of God. The angel assures Paul of his safety and destiny to stand before Caesar.

Believer, even in the midst of life's storms and uncertainties, remember that God's angels stand by you. They bring messages of assurance, guidance, and destiny. Trust in God's plan, for He has a purpose for your life that transcends the challenges you may face.

Revelation 1:1 - The revelation of Jesus Christ, which God gave unto him, to shew unto his servants things which must shortly come to pass; and he sent by his angel unto his servant John:

In the opening verse of the book of Revelation, we find the angel delivering the revelation of Jesus Christ to the apostle John. This unveiling of future events holds significance for the entire Church.

Believer, the same God who revealed His plan to John through an angel desire to reveal His truths to you. Be diligent in seeking God's revelation through His Word and prayer, for angels are often involved in conveying His divine messages.

As we explore how angels aid in unveiling the mysteries of God, let us internalize these truths and apply them to our personal lives:

1. Persistent seeking: Like Jacob, persistently seek God's blessings and revelations, even in the midst of wrestling with the mysteries of faith.

2. Guardians of God's presence: Recognize the role of angels as guardians of God's presence and mercy. Approach God's presence with reverence, knowing that angels accompany you.

3. Divine interceptors: Be open to divine interventions that may redirect your path when you are headed in the wrong direction, just as Balaam experienced.

4. Swift responders: Understand that angels are swift to respond to your prayers, providing insight, skill, and understanding in the mysteries of God's will.

5. Beloved and favored: Embrace God's love and favor upon your life, as seen in His interactions with Daniel and Mary. You are greatly beloved, and He desires to reveal His plans to you.

6. Unexpected revelations: When faced with troubling or perplexing situations, trust that God's favor and His divine plan may be at work, even if it seems unexpected.

7. Assurance in the storm: In the midst of life's challenges, find comfort in the presence of God's angels, who bring messages of assurance, guidance, and destiny.

8. Seek divine revelation: Like John, diligently seek God's revelation through His Word and prayer, knowing that angels are involved in conveying His divine messages.

Believer, the mysteries of God are not meant to remain shrouded in obscurity. Through the ministry of angels, God unveils His truths and purposes to those who seek Him with a humble and open heart. May you be steadfast in your pursuit of God's mysteries, and may the angels of the Lord continue to aid in revealing the depths of His love and wisdom in your life.

Chapter Seven

―・―◇―・―

Discerning the Signs of Angelic Presence

In the timeline of our lives, angels move among us, often unnoticed but ever-present. These celestial beings bear messages and fulfill divine assignments, carrying out the will of the Almighty. As we journey together to unveil the signs of angelic presence, we shall draw wisdom and inspiration from the timeless words of the King James Version of the Bible. But this exploration is not mere curiosity; it is an invitation to discern the signs of angelic presence in our personal lives and to recognize that the heavenly realm is closer than we often realize.

Genesis 16:7-8 - And the angel of the Lord found her by a fountain of water in the wilderness, by the fountain in the way to Shur. And he said, Hagar, Sarai's maid, whence camest thou? and whither wilt thou go? And she said, I flee from the face of my mistress Sarai.

Our journey begins with Hagar, a woman fleeing from hardship. In the wilderness, she encounters the angel of the Lord by a fountain of water. The angel's inquiry reveals his awareness of her situation.

Believer, this account reminds us that angels are attentive to our circumstances, even in our moments of distress. In times of wilderness and despair, be open to the possibility of angelic encounters. Angels may be near, ready to guide and comfort you.

Genesis 28:12 - And he dreamed, and behold a ladder set up on the earth, and the top of it reached to heaven: and behold the angels of God ascending and descending on it.

In Jacob's dream, he witnesses a ladder stretching from earth to heaven, with angels ascending and descending. This remarkable vision unveils the connection between heaven and earth.

Believer, this dream underscores the accessibility of God's heavenly realm. Angels are the messengers who traverse this celestial bridge, bringing God's messages and guidance to us. Be mindful that your prayers and petitions can reach the throne of God through the ministry of angels.

Exodus 3:2-4 - And the angel of the Lord appeared unto him in a flame of fire out of the midst of a bush: and he looked, and, behold, the bush burned with fire, and the bush was not consumed. And Moses said, I will now turn aside, and see this great sight, why the bush is not burnt. And when the Lord saw that he turned aside to see, God called unto him out of the midst of the bush, and said, Moses, Moses. And he said, Here am I.

Moses' encounter with the burning bush reveals the angel of the Lord's presence. The bush, aflame but not consumed, draws Moses' curiosity, prompting him to turn aside.

Believer, this account teaches us that angelic presence can manifest in extraordinary ways, capturing our attention and beckoning us to draw near. When you encounter moments of wonder and awe, be receptive to the divine message that may follow, as God calls you to His presence.

Judges 6:11-12 - And there came an angel of the Lord, and sat under an oak which was in Ophrah, that pertained unto Joash the Abiezrite: and his son Gideon threshed wheat by the winepress, to hide it from the Midianites. And the angel of the Lord appeared unto him, and said unto him, The Lord is with thee, thou mighty man of valour.

Gideon's encounter with the angel of the Lord is a classic example of discerning angelic presence. Gideon initially perceives the angel as a stranger, but the angel's message reveals his true identity.

Believer, this narrative underscores the importance of discernment. Sometimes, angelic presence may be veiled in ordinary circumstances or people. Be open to the possibility that God's messengers may be in your midst, bearing messages of courage and purpose.

Daniel 10:10-12 - And, behold, an hand touched me, which set me upon my knees and upon the palms of my hands. And he said unto me, O Daniel, a man greatly beloved, understand the words that I speak unto thee, and stand upright: for unto thee am I now sent. And when he had spoken this word unto me, I stood trembling. Then said he unto me, Fear not, Daniel: for from the first day that thou didst set thine heart to understand, and to chasten thyself before thy God, thy words were heard, and I am come for thy words.

In Daniel's vision, he encounters an angelic being who touches him and addresses him as "a man greatly beloved." The angel reassures Daniel, explaining that he was sent in response to Daniel's prayers.

Believer, this passage highlights the direct connection between our prayers and the angelic realm. When you set your heart to understand God's will and seek His presence through prayer, rest assured that angels are dispatched to respond to your words. Trust that your prayers are heard, and angelic aid is at hand.

Matthew 28:5-7 - And the angel answered and said unto the women, Fear not ye: for I know that ye seek Jesus, which was crucified. He is not here: for he is risen, as he said. Come, see the place where the Lord lay. And go quickly, and tell his disciples that he is risen from the dead; and, behold, he goeth before you into Galilee; there shall ye see him: lo, I have told you.

The resurrection of Jesus is a momentous event accompanied by the presence of angels. When the women visit the empty tomb, they encounter an angel who assures them of Christ's resurrection and instructs them to share the news with the disciples.

Believer, this encounter serves as a reminder that angels often bear messages of hope and revelation, especially in moments of profound significance. When you seek the risen Christ, anticipate angelic presence and messages that confirm His resurrection power in your life.

Acts 12:6-7 - And when Herod would have brought him forth, the same night Peter was sleeping between two soldiers, bound with two chains: and the keepers before the door kept the prison. And, behold, the angel of the Lord came upon him, and a light shined in the prison: and he smote Peter on the side, and raised him up, saying, Arise up quickly. And his chains fell off from his hands.

In the darkest hour of Peter's imprisonment, an angel of the Lord appears, illuminating the prison cell and setting Peter free from his chains.

Believer, this account reminds us that angels can manifest in times of confinement and darkness, bringing liberation and divine illumination. When you find yourself bound by chains of adversity or despair, be vigilant for the light of angelic presence and the release they bring.

Hebrews 13:2 - Be not forgetful to entertain strangers: for thereby some have entertained angels unawares.

The writer of Hebrews issues a poignant reminder: we should not be forgetful to entertain strangers, for in doing so, some have entertained angels without realizing it.

Believer, this verse emphasizes the importance of hospitality and openness to the unexpected. Angels may come in the guise of strangers, and our kindness toward them can lead to divine encounters. Be attentive to the needs of those around you, for in serving others, you may unknowingly host angels.

As we discern the signs of angelic presence, let us internalize these truths and apply them to our personal lives:

1. Awareness in adversity: In moments of distress and wilderness, be open to the possibility of angelic encounters. Angels may be near, ready to guide and comfort you.

2. Accessible heavenly realm: Recognize that God's heavenly realm is within reach, and angels serve as messengers between heaven and earth. Your prayers and petitions can traverse this celestial bridge.

3. Extraordinary manifestations: Be receptive to extraordinary manifestations, like Jacob's ladder or the burning bush, as they may signal the presence of angels and God's call to His presence.

4. Discernment of strangers: Practice discernment in your interactions with others, for angelic presence may be veiled in ordinary circumstances or people. Be open to messages of courage and purpose.

5. Connection between prayer and angels: Understand the direct connection between your prayers and the angelic realm. Trust that your prayers are heard, and angelic aid is dispatched in response.

6. Messages of hope and revelation: Anticipate angelic presence and messages in moments of profound significance, such as the resurrection of Christ, that confirm His power and presence in your life.

7. Liberation from darkness: Be vigilant for the light of angelic presence in times of confinement or despair. Angels bring liberation and divine illumination to dispel darkness.

8. Hospitality and kindness: Practice hospitality and kindness, for in serving others, you may unknowingly host angels. Be attentive to the needs of those around you, recognizing that your interactions may lead to divine encounters.

Believer, may you walk in the awareness of angelic presence, discerning the signs that surround you in your daily life. The heavenly realm is not distant; it is intertwined with our earthly journey. As you discern the signs, may you draw closer to the divine mysteries and the ever-present guidance of God's messengers, the angels.

Chapter Eight

――・・◇・・――

Guidelines for Interacting with Angels

As we journey deeper into the realm of angels, it is crucial to recognize that our interactions with these celestial beings are governed by divine principles and guidelines. While the presence of angels can bring comfort, guidance, and revelation, it is imperative that we approach these encounters with reverence and wisdom. In this chapter, we will explore the biblical guidelines for interacting with angels, drawing wisdom and inspiration from the timeless words of the King James Version of the Bible. These guidelines are not merely academic; they are meant to be applied to the believer's personal life, ensuring that our encounters with angels align with God's divine plan.

Hebrews 1:14 - Are they not all ministering spirits, sent forth to minister for them who shall be heirs of salvation?

The writer of Hebrews reminds us that angels are ministering spirits, sent by God to serve and assist those who will inherit salvation.

Believer, the first guideline is to approach angelic encounters with humility and reverence. Angels are sent by God to minister to us, and their purpose is to assist in our journey of salvation. When you encounter an angel, recognize that it is a sacred moment and receive their ministry with gratitude.

Exodus 20:3-5 - Thou shalt have no other gods before me. Thou shalt not make unto thee any graven image, or any likeness of any thing that is in heaven above, or that is in the earth beneath, or that is in the water under the earth: Thou shalt not bow down thyself to them, nor serve them: for I the Lord thy God am a jealous God, visiting the iniquity of the fathers upon the children unto the third and fourth generation of them that hate me.

The second guideline stems from the Ten Commandments, emphasizing the importance of worshiping the one true God and refraining from idolatry.

Believer, when encountering angels, remember that they are not to be worshiped or revered above God. They are messengers and servants of the Most High. Maintain your devotion and worship exclusively for God, giving Him the honor and reverence, He deserves.

Colossians 2:18 - Let no man beguile you of your reward in a voluntary humility and worshipping of angels, intruding into those things which he hath not seen, vainly puffed up by his fleshly mind.

Paul's letter to the Colossians issues a warning against being deceived by those who advocate the worship of angels and engage in unauthorized spiritual experiences.

Believer, the third guideline is to exercise discernment in spiritual matters. Beware of individuals or teachings that promote the worship or excessive veneration of angels. Do not be beguiled into pursuing sensational or mystical experiences that are not grounded in the Word of God.

1 Corinthians 14:33 - For God is not the author of confusion, but of peace, as in all churches of the saints.

The apostle Paul emphasizes the importance of order and peace in the church.

Believer, the fourth guideline is to seek clarity and order in your interactions with angels. God is not the author of confusion. When encountering angelic presence or messages, seek confirmation through prayer, the Word of God, and wise counsel from mature believers. Ensure that your experiences align with God's divine order and peace.

Matthew 18:10 - Take heed that ye despise not one of these little ones; for I say unto you, That in heaven their angels do always behold the face of my Father which is in heaven.

In the Gospel of Matthew, Jesus speaks of the angels of children who have a direct connection with the Father in heaven.

Believer, the fifth guideline reminds us of the special care and watchfulness that angels have over children. When interacting with children or ministering to them, be mindful of the angels who are always in the presence of God. Treat children with love, respect, and kindness, recognizing the divine guardianship that surrounds them.

Acts 10:3-4 - He saw in a vision evidently about the ninth hour of the day an angel of God coming in to him, and saying unto him, Cornelius. And when he looked on him, he was afraid, and said, What is it, Lord? And he said unto him, Thy prayers and thine alms are come up for a memorial before God.

In the account of Cornelius, a Gentile centurion, he receives a visitation from an angel who acknowledges his prayers and charitable deeds.

Believer, the sixth guideline encourages us to continue in prayer, righteousness, and acts of kindness. Just as Cornelius' prayers and alms ascended as a memorial before God, our sincere prayers and righteous living attract the attention of heaven. Be faithful in your devotion to God, and let your actions be a fragrant offering that captures the notice of angels.

Hebrews 13:2 - Be not forgetful to entertain strangers: for thereby some have entertained angels unawares.

The writer of Hebrews reminds us to show hospitality to strangers, as some have unknowingly hosted angels.

Believer, the seventh guideline encourages us to be hospitable and kind-hearted to strangers. Recognize that your interactions with others, even those you consider strangers, may lead to divine encounters. Extend the love of Christ to all, for in doing so, you may unknowingly entertain angels.

1 Thessalonians 5:19-21 - Quench not the Spirit. Despise not prophesyings. Prove all things; hold fast that which is good.

In his letter to the Thessalonians, Paul advises against quenching the Spirit, despising prophesies, and encourages testing and holding onto what is good.

Believer, the eighth guideline is to remain open to the work of the Holy Spirit and the prophetic. While discernment is crucial, do not quench the Spirit by dismissing all spiritual experiences or messages. Instead, test all things, holding fast to what aligns with the truth of God's Word.

Matthew 6:9-10 - After this manner therefore pray ye: Our Father which art in heaven, Hallowed be thy name. Thy kingdom come. Thy will be done in earth, as it is in heaven.

In the Lord's Prayer, Jesus teaches His disciples to pray for God's kingdom to come and His will to be done on earth as it is in heaven.

Believer, the ninth guideline is to align your prayers with the heavenly realm. As you pray for God's will to be done on earth, invite angelic assistance in bringing about God's kingdom purposes. Seek alignment with heaven in your prayers, trusting that angels are active agents in fulfilling God's divine plan.

James 4:7 - Submit yourselves therefore to God. Resist the devil, and he will flee from you.

James encourages believers to submit to God and resist the devil, knowing that the devil will flee.

Believer, the tenth guideline is to maintain spiritual discernment and resistance. While angels are messengers of God, it is crucial to discern the source of any spiritual encounter. If an encounter or message contradicts God's Word or promotes ungodly behavior, resist it firmly and cling to the truth of Scripture.

As we explore these guidelines for interacting with angels, let us internalize these truths and apply them to our personal lives:

1. Approach with humility and reverence: Receive angelic encounters with humility and reverence, recognizing their role as ministering spirits sent by God to assist in your journey of salvation.

2. Worship God alone: Maintain exclusive worship and reverence for the one true God. Do not idolize or worship angels or any other created being.

3. Exercise discernment: Beware of teachings or individuals promoting the excessive veneration of angels or encouraging unauthorized spiritual experiences. Be discerning in spiritual matters.

4. Seek clarity and order: Pursue clarity and divine order in your interactions with angels. Seek confirmation through prayer, Scripture, and wise counsel.

5. Care for children: Recognize the special care and watchfulness of angels over children. Treat children with love, respect, and kindness, acknowledging the divine guardianship that surrounds them.

6. Continue in prayer and righteousness: Maintain a life of prayer, righteousness, and acts of kindness. Let your prayers and deeds ascend as a memorial before God, attracting the attention of heaven.

7. Show hospitality: Extend hospitality and kindness to strangers, for in doing so, you may unknowingly host angels. Be open to divine encounters through acts of love.

8. Remain open to the Spirit: Do not quench the Holy Spirit or despise prophetic messages. Test all things, holding fast to what aligns with God's Word.

9. Align your prayers with heaven: Pray for God's kingdom to come and His will to be done on earth as it is in heaven. Invite angelic assistance in bringing about God's divine purposes.

10. Maintain spiritual discernment and resistance: Be vigilant in discerning the source of spiritual encounters. Resist any message or experience that contradicts God's Word or promotes ungodliness.

Believer, may these guidelines serve as a compass in your interactions with angels. As you navigate the celestial realm, may you do so with wisdom, reverence, and a steadfast commitment to aligning with God's divine plan. May your encounters with angels be marked by a deepening of your faith and a greater understanding of the heavenly realm's role in your earthly journey.

Chapter Nine

Unveiling the Unfathomable Depths of God's Mysterious Realm

In the pages of Scripture, we embark on a journey to explore the unfathomable depths of God's mysterious realm—an ethereal tapestry woven with divine beings, including angels. These celestial messengers carry out God's will in ways that often leave us in awe and wonder. As we venture deeper into this enigmatic realm, we seek to draw wisdom and inspiration from the timeless words of the King James Version of the Bible. These revelations are not distant or abstract; they are meant to be applied to the believer's personal life, bringing us closer to the awe-inspiring mysteries of God.

1 Corinthians 2:9-10 - But as it is written, Eye hath not seen, nor ear heard, neither have entered into the heart of man, the things which God hath prepared for them that love him. But God hath revealed them unto us by his Spirit: for the Spirit searcheth all things, yea, the deep things of God.

The apostle Paul reminds us that our human senses cannot fathom the depths of God's mysteries. However, God has chosen to reveal these profound truths to us through His Spirit, who searches the deep things of God.

Believer, our journey begins with the realization that the mysteries of God's realm are not hidden from us. Through the Holy Spirit, God unveils His profound truths and secrets to those who love Him. Be open to the Spirit's leading, for He is the key to understanding the unfathomable depths of God's enigmatic realm.

Isaiah 6:1-3 - In the year that king Uzziah died I saw also the Lord sitting upon a throne, high and lifted up, and his train filled the temple. Above it stood the seraphims: each one had six wings; with twain he covered his face, and with twain he covered his feet, and with twain he did fly. And one cried unto another, and said, Holy, holy, holy, is the Lord of hosts: the whole earth is full of his glory.

Isaiah's vision takes us to the throne room of heaven, where the Lord sits in majestic splendor, surrounded by seraphim who cry out, "Holy, holy, holy is the Lord of hosts."

Believer, this vision unveils the holiness and glory of God's realm. The second revelation is that the heavenly realm is a place of unparalleled holiness and divine splendor. As we explore this unfathomable realm, let us strive for holiness in our own lives and recognize that God's glory fills the earth.

Ezekiel 1:4-5, 10-11 - And I looked, and, behold, a whirlwind came out of the north, a great cloud, and a fire infolding itself, and a brightness was about it, and out of the midst thereof as the colour of amber, out of the midst of the fire. Also out of the midst thereof came the likeness of four living creatures. And this was their

appearance; they had the likeness of a man. As for the likeness of their faces, they four had the face of a man, and the face of a lion, on the right side: and they four had the face of an ox on the left side; they four also had the face of an eagle. And their faces and their wings were stretched upward; two wings of every one were joined one to another, and two covered their bodies.

Ezekiel's vision introduces us to four living creatures with the likeness of a man, a lion, an ox, and an eagle, each with four faces and wings stretched upward.

Believer, this vision underscores the diversity and complexity of the heavenly realm. The third revelation is that God's unfathomable realm is filled with diverse and awe-inspiring beings. Embrace the diversity of God's creation and recognize that His mysteries are beyond our human comprehension.

Daniel 10:12 - Then said he unto me, Fear not, Daniel: for from the first day that thou didst set thine heart to understand, and to chasten thyself before thy God, thy words were heard, and I am come for thy words.

In Daniel's encounter with an angel, he receives a message of assurance. The angel tells Daniel that from the moment he set his heart to understand and humbled himself before God, his words were heard, and the angel was dispatched.

Believer, the fourth revelation is that God responds to our heart's desire to understand His mysteries. From the moment we set our hearts to seek Him and humble ourselves, He hears our words, and His divine messengers are dispatched to bring understanding. When you seek to unveil the unfathomable depths of God's realm, do so with a heart set on understanding and humility.

Revelation 4:1-3 - After this I looked, and, behold, a door was opened in heaven: and the first voice which I heard was as it were of a trumpet talking with me; which said, Come up hither, and I will show thee things which must be hereafter. And immediately I was in the spirit: and, behold, a throne was set in heaven, and one sat on the throne. And he that sat was to look upon like a jasper and a sardine stone: and there was a rainbow round about the throne, in sight like unto an emerald.

John's vision in Revelation transports him to the heavenly realm through an open door. He sees a glorious throne and One who sits on it, described in dazzling terms.

Believer, the fifth revelation is that God invites us to enter into the heavenly realm and witness the unfolding of His divine plan. When we engage with God's unfathomable realm, we can expect to encounter His glory and sovereignty. Be open to the call to come up higher and experience the mysteries of God's realm.

Revelation 5:11-12 - And I beheld, and I heard the voice of many angels round about the throne and the beasts and the elders: and the number of them was ten thousand times ten thousand, and thousands of thousands; Saying with a loud voice, Worthy is the Lamb that was slain to receive power, and riches, and wisdom, and strength, and honour, and glory, and blessing.

John's vision continues as he witnesses the multitude of angels praising the Lamb who was slain, declaring His worthiness to receive power, riches, wisdom, strength, honor, glory, and blessing.

Believer, the sixth revelation is that the heavenly realm resounds with worship and adoration of the Lamb of God. As we journey deeper into God's unfathomable realm, let us cultivate a heart of worship, recognizing the worthiness of Jesus Christ to receive our praise and adoration.

Revelation 21:1-2 - And I saw a new heaven and a new earth: for the first heaven and the first earth were passed away; and there was no more sea. And I John saw the holy city, new Jerusalem, coming down from God out of heaven, prepared as a bride adorned for her husband.

In the closing chapters of Revelation, John envisions a new heaven and a new earth, and the holy city, the new Jerusalem, descending from God out of heaven.

Believer, the seventh revelation is that God's unfathomable realm holds the promise of a new heaven and a new earth. As we explore the depths of God's mysteries, let us eagerly anticipate the fulfillment of God's promises, knowing that one day, we will dwell in the heavenly city, the new Jerusalem.

As we unveil the unfathomable depths of God's mysterious realm, let us internalize these truths and apply them to our personal lives:

1. The Holy Spirit as our guide: Recognize the Holy Spirit as the revealer of God's mysteries. Be open to His leading and guidance as you seek to understand the unfathomable depths of God's enigmatic realm.

2. Pursuit of holiness and reverence: Strive for holiness in your life, recognizing the profound holiness and glory of God's heavenly realm.

3. Embrace diversity: Embrace the diversity and complexity of God's creation, acknowledging that His mysteries are beyond human comprehension.

4. Humility and seeking: Approach God's mysteries with humility and a heart set on understanding. Know that God responds

to your desire to know Him and unveils His mysteries to those who seek Him.

5. Invitation to enter: Be open to God's invitation to enter into the heavenly realm and witness the unfolding of His divine plan.

6. Cultivate a heart of worship: Recognize the worthiness of Jesus Christ to receive your praise and adoration. Cultivate a heart of worship as you journey deeper into God's unfathomable realm.

7. Anticipation of God's promises: Eagerly anticipate the fulfillment of God's promises, including the new heaven and new earth. Live with the hope that one day, you will dwell in the heavenly city, the new Jerusalem.

Believer, as we unveil the unfathomable depths of God's mysterious realm, may your faith be deepened, your understanding expanded, and your heart filled with awe and wonder. The mysteries of God are meant to draw us closer to Him, and as we journey together into His unfathomable realm, may we be transformed by the profound truths that await us.

Chapter Ten

Cultivating a Lifestyle of Seeking God's Mysteries

In the quiet moments of reflection and contemplation, have you ever wondered about the mysteries that lie just beyond the grasp of our understanding? These mysteries are the very essence of God's enigmatic realm, and they beckon us to delve deeper into the profound depths of His presence. Angels, those celestial beings who traverse the boundary between heaven and earth, offer us a glimpse into this wondrous realm. In this chapter, we will embark on a journey to cultivate a lifestyle of seeking God's mysteries, drawing wisdom and inspiration from the timeless words of the King James Version of the Bible. These revelations are not mere intellectual pursuits; they are meant to be applied to the believer's personal life, transforming us into seekers of God's profound mysteries.

Proverbs 25:2 - It is the glory of God to conceal a thing: but the honour of kings is to search out a matter.

The Book of Proverbs reminds us that it is the glory of God to conceal things, but the honor of kings is to search out matters.

Believer, the first revelation is that seeking out God's mysteries is an honorable pursuit. Just as kings are honored by seeking out hidden matters, we, as children of the Most High, are called to explore the concealed truths of God's enigmatic realm. It is a pursuit that brings honor to our relationship with the King of Kings.

Jeremiah 33:3 - Call unto me, and I will answer thee, and shew thee great and mighty things, which thou knowest not.

In the words of the prophet Jeremiah, God invites us to call upon Him, promising to answer and reveal great and mighty things that we do not know.

Believer, the second revelation is that God is the ultimate revealer of mysteries. When we earnestly seek Him and call upon His name, He responds by unveiling profound truths and insights that surpass our human understanding. Cultivate a lifestyle of seeking God through prayer, for in His presence, mysteries are unraveled.

Matthew 7:7-8 - Ask, and it shall be given you; seek, and ye shall find; knock, and it shall be opened unto you: For every one that asketh receiveth; and he that seeketh findeth; and to him that knocketh it shall be opened.

In the Gospel of Matthew, Jesus instructs us to ask, seek, and knock, promising that those who do will receive, find, and have doors opened to them.

Believer, the third revelation is that persistence in seeking God's mysteries yields results. Jesus encourages us to keep asking, keep seeking, and keep knocking. A lifestyle of persistent seeking is a key to unlocking the hidden treasures of God's realm.

Psalm 25:14 - The secret of the Lord is with them that fear him; and he will shew them his covenant.

The psalmist reminds us that the secret of the Lord is with those who fear Him, and He reveals His covenant to them.

Believer, the fourth revelation is that cultivating a healthy reverence and awe of God is essential to understanding His mysteries. When we fear the Lord in a way that recognizes His majesty and holiness, He entrusts us with the secrets of His covenant. It is in this intimate relationship that mysteries are unveiled.

1 Corinthians 14:2 - For he that speaketh in an unknown tongue speaketh not unto men, but unto God: for no man understandeth him; howbeit in the spirit he speaketh mysteries.

In Paul's first letter to the Corinthians, he explains that speaking in tongues allows a person to speak mysteries in the spirit, not understood by others but communicated directly to God.

Believer, the fifth revelation is that there are spiritual dimensions to seeking God's mysteries. Speaking in tongues is one-way believers can engage in spiritual communication with God, allowing the Spirit to reveal mysteries beyond human comprehension. Cultivate a lifestyle of spiritual sensitivity and expression.

Colossians 2:2-3 - That their hearts might be comforted, being knit together in love, and unto all riches of the full assurance of understanding, to the acknowledgement of the mystery of God, and of the Father, and of Christ; In whom are hid all the treasures of wisdom and knowledge.

The apostle Paul writes to the Colossians, expressing his desire for their hearts to be comforted and filled with understanding, particularly in acknowledging the mystery of God and the treasures of wisdom and knowledge hidden in Christ.

Believer, the sixth revelation is that Christ Himself holds the key to unraveling God's mysteries. In Him are hidden all the treasures of wisdom and knowledge. Cultivate a lifestyle of deepening your relationship with Christ, for in Him, you will find the answers to the profound mysteries of God.

Ephesians 1:17-18 - That the God of our Lord Jesus Christ, the Father of glory, may give unto you the spirit of wisdom and revelation in the knowledge of him: The eyes of your understanding being enlightened; that ye may know what is the hope of his calling, and what the riches of the glory of his inheritance in the saints.

In his letter to the Ephesians, Paul prays for believers to receive the spirit of wisdom and revelation in the knowledge of God, that their understanding may be enlightened to know the hope of His calling and the riches of His inheritance in the saints.

Believer, the seventh revelation is that God desires to grant us a spirit of wisdom and revelation. Through this spiritual enlightenment, we can gain insight into the hope of God's calling and the glorious inheritance He has prepared for His saints. Cultivate a lifestyle of prayer, asking God to open the eyes of your understanding.

Romans 11:33 - O the depth of the riches both of the wisdom and knowledge of God! how unsearchable are his judgments, and his ways past finding out!

The apostle Paul, in his letter to the Romans, exclaims at the depth of God's wisdom and knowledge, acknowledging the unsearchable nature of His judgments and ways.

Believer, the eighth revelation is that while we seek God's mysteries, there will always be aspects of His wisdom and judgments that remain beyond our full comprehension. It is in recognizing the depth of God's wisdom that we embrace the humility of seeking, knowing that there will always be more to discover.

1 Corinthians 13:12 - For now we see through a glass, darkly; but then face to face: now I know in part; but then shall I know even as also I am known.

Paul, in his first letter to the Corinthians, describes our current understanding of God's mysteries as seeing through a glass darkly, but he anticipates a time when we shall know even as we are known.

Believer, the ninth revelation is that our journey of seeking God's mysteries is progressive. While we may have limited understanding now, there is a future where we will know fully, just as God knows us completely. Cultivate a lifestyle of patient and persistent seeking, knowing that the journey is as important as the destination.

Psalm 119:105 - Thy word is a lamp unto my feet, and a light unto my path.

The psalmist declares that God's Word is a lamp to our feet and a light to our path.

Believer, the tenth revelation is that the Word of God is our guiding light in the pursuit of His mysteries. As we cultivate a lifestyle of seeking, let the Scriptures be the lamp that illuminates our path, leading us deeper into the profound depths of God's presence.

Believer, as we seek to cultivate a lifestyle of seeking God's mysteries, may you be encouraged to embark on a journey filled with honor, spiritual sensitivity, and a deepening relationship with Christ. Know that the pursuit of God's profound mysteries is not only a noble endeavor but also a transformative one.

Chapter Eleven

―――・・◇・・―――

The Role of Angels in Eschatology

As we journey through the pages of "Angels Unveiled," we've explored the celestial realm, encountered angelic beings, and unveiled the mysteries of God's enigmatic realm. Yet, there's another dimension to the role of angels that we must delve into—their significance in eschatology. Eschatology, the study of end times, invites us to consider how angels play a vital role in the fulfillment of God's ultimate plan. In this chapter, we will embark on a journey to uncover the profound role of angels in eschatology, drawing wisdom and inspiration from the timeless words of the King James Version of the Bible. These revelations are not abstract; they are meant to be applied to the believer's personal life, providing guidance, hope, and purpose in these last days.

Matthew 13:39 - The enemy that sowed them is the devil; the harvest is the end of the world; and the reapers are the angels.

In the parable of the wheat and tares, Jesus reveals a profound truth about the end times. He explains that at the end of the world, the reapers are the angels.

Believer, the first revelation is that angels are intimately involved in the final harvest. Just as they played a role in sowing the seeds of God's kingdom, they will also participate in the gathering of souls at the end of the age. This truth reminds us of the urgency of our mission—to spread the gospel and lead others into God's kingdom.

Matthew 24:31 - And he shall send his angels with a great sound of a trumpet, and they shall gather together his elect from the four winds, from one end of heaven to the other.

In the discourse on the end times, Jesus speaks of a day when He will send His angels with a great sound of a trumpet to gather His elect from all corners of the earth.

Believer, the second revelation is that angels will play a crucial role in the gathering of God's chosen ones. This passage offers hope and assurance to believers, assuring us that God's heavenly messengers will be instrumental in our final gathering to Him. Let this truth strengthen your faith and anticipation of Christ's return.

Revelation 8:3-5 - And another angel came and stood at the altar, having a golden censer; and there was given unto him much incense, that he should offer it with the prayers of all saints upon the golden altar which was before the throne. And the smoke of the incense, which came with the prayers of the saints, ascended up before God out of the angel's hand. And the angel took the censer, and filled it with fire of the altar, and cast it into the earth: and there were voices, and thunderings, and lightnings, and an earthquake.

In the book of Revelation, we encounter an angel who stands at the altar with a golden censer. This angel offers incense with the prayers of the saints, and the smoke of the incense ascends before God. The angel then casts fire from the altar to the earth, resulting in dramatic events.

Believer, the third revelation is that angels serve as mediators of our prayers before God. Our prayers, like incense, rise before the heavenly altar, and angels are involved in this sacred process. The response to the angel's actions underscores the significance of our prayers in the unfolding of end-time events. Let this truth inspire you to persist in prayer and intercession, knowing that your prayers have a powerful impact on the course of history.

Revelation 14:6-7 - And I saw another angel fly in the midst of heaven, having the everlasting gospel to preach unto them that dwell on the earth, and to every nation, and kindred, and tongue, and people, Saying with a loud voice, Fear God, and give glory to him; for the hour of his judgment is come: and worship him that made heaven, and earth, and the sea, and the fountains of waters.

In the book of Revelation, John witnesses another angel flying in the midst of heaven, proclaiming the everlasting gospel to all the inhabitants of the earth.

Believer, the fourth revelation is that angels will be messengers of the gospel even during the end times. Their role in proclaiming the good news highlights the urgency of sharing the message of salvation with the world. Let this truth motivate you to be a faithful witness of Christ, knowing that angels join us in this mission.

Revelation 16:5-7 - And I heard the angel of the waters say, Thou art righteous, O Lord, which art, and wast, and shalt be, because thou hast judged thus. For they have shed the blood of saints and prophets, and thou hast given them blood to drink; for they are worthy. And I heard another out of the altar say, Even so, Lord God Almighty, true and righteous are thy judgments.

In the book of Revelation, John hears an angel speaking about the righteousness of God's judgments, particularly regarding those who have persecuted the saints and prophets.

Believer, the fifth revelation is that angels bear witness to the righteousness of God's judgments. Even in times of tribulation and persecution, we are reminded that God's judgments are just and righteous. This truth encourages us to trust in God's sovereignty, even in the midst of difficult circumstances.

Revelation 19:10 - And I fell at his feet to worship him. And he said unto me, See thou do it not: I am thy fellowservant, and of thy brethren that have the testimony of Jesus: worship God: for the testimony of Jesus is the spirit of prophecy.

In the book of Revelation, John encounters an angel and falls at his feet to worship him. However, the angel redirects John's worship toward God, emphasizing that he is a fellow servant and that the testimony of Jesus is the spirit of prophecy.

Believer, the sixth revelation is that angels themselves point us to worship God. They understand the centrality of Jesus in the prophetic message and redirect our focus to the One who is worthy of all worship. Let this truth remind you to worship God wholeheartedly, for He alone is the source of our hope and the fulfillment of all prophecy.

Revelation 22:8-9 - And I John saw these things, and heard them. And when I had heard and seen, I fell down to worship before the feet of the angel which shewed me these things. Then saith he unto me, See thou do it not: for I am thy fellowservant, and of thy brethren the prophets, and of them which keep the sayings of this book: worship God.

In the closing verses of the book of Revelation, John once again falls down to worship an angel who had shown him these things. However, the angel, like before, redirects John's worship toward God, emphasizing their shared role as servants and the importance of worshiping God.

Believer, the seventh revelation is that angels consistently redirect our worship toward God. They serve alongside us as fellow servants in God's divine plan, and they remind us of the centrality of worshiping the Almighty. Let this truth inspire you to cultivate a lifestyle of worship, for in the presence of God, we find hope and purpose in the midst of eschatological events.

May you now contemplate the role of angels in eschatology, may you be encouraged to embrace your role as a fellow servant of God in these last days. Angels serve as messengers, harvesters, and witnesses to God's righteousness and judgments. They remind us of the urgency of our mission, the power of our prayers, and the centrality of worshiping God. As we navigate the complexities of the end times, let these revelations empower you to live a life of purpose, hope, and unwavering faith in the One who holds the future in His hands.

Chapter Twelve

Angelic Involvement in Judgment

As we continue our journey through the pages of "Angels Unveiled," we come to a chapter that explores a profound and often misunderstood aspect of angelic activity—their involvement in judgment. In the course of God's divine plan, angels serve as both messengers of mercy and agents of justice. In this chapter, we will embark on a journey to understand the role of angels in judgment, drawing wisdom and inspiration from the timeless words of the King James Version of the Bible. These revelations are not meant to instill fear but to provide clarity on the divine order of justice and the believer's response to it.

Genesis 19:1, 12-13, 24-25 - And there came two angels to Sodom at even; and Lot sat in the gate of Sodom: and Lot seeing them rose up to meet them; and he bowed himself with his face toward the ground. And the men said unto Lot, Hast thou here any besides? son in law, and thy sons, and thy daughters, and whatsoever thou hast in the city; bring them out of this place: For we will

destroy this place because the cry of them is waxen great before the face of the Lord; and the Lord hath sent us to destroy it. Then the Lord rained upon Sodom and upon Gomorrah brimstone and fire from the Lord out of heaven; And he overthrew those cities, and all the plain, and all the inhabitants of the cities, and that which grew upon the ground.

In the narrative of Sodom and Gomorrah, two angels visit Lot and deliver a message of impending judgment. They warn Lot to gather his family and flee the city before its destruction.

Believer, the first revelation is that angels are often God's messengers of impending judgment. Their role is to deliver warnings and opportunities for repentance. In this story, we see the urgency of heeding divine warnings and escaping the consequences of sin. Let this truth remind you of the importance of heeding God's warnings in your own life and responding with repentance.

Exodus 12:23 - For the Lord will pass through to smite the Egyptians; and when he seeth the blood upon the lintel, and on the two side posts, the Lord will pass over the door, and will not suffer the destroyer to come in unto your houses to smite you.

During the Passover in Egypt, God sent the destroyer to strike down the firstborn of the Egyptians. However, the Israelites were instructed to mark their doorposts with the blood of a lamb, and the Lord would pass over their houses, sparing them from judgment.

Believer, the second revelation is that angels are sometimes involved in executing God's judgment. However, there is a way to be protected from that judgment—by the blood of the Lamb. Just as the Israelites were spared through the blood of a lamb, we are saved through the blood of Jesus Christ. Embrace the protection and redemption offered by the blood of the Lamb.

2 Samuel 24:15-16 - So the Lord sent a pestilence upon Israel from the morning even to the time appointed: and there died of the people from Dan even to Beer-sheba seventy thousand men. And when the angel stretched out his hand upon Jerusalem to destroy it, the Lord repented him of the evil, and said to the angel that destroyed the people, It is enough: stay now thine hand. And the angel of the Lord was by the threshing place of Araunah the Jebusite.

In 2 Samuel, we read of a pestilence that God sent upon Israel as a judgment. An angel was poised to destroy Jerusalem, but God relented and commanded the angel to stop.

Believer, the third revelation is that God's judgments are executed with precision and purpose. Even in the midst of judgment, God is merciful and responsive to repentance. The presence of angels in this narrative reminds us of the divine balance between justice and mercy. Let this truth encourage you to turn to God in repentance, knowing that His mercy is available even in times of judgment.

2 Kings 19:35 - And it came to pass that night, that the angel of the Lord went out, and smote in the camp of the Assyrians an hundred fourscore and five thousand: and when they arose early in the morning, behold, they were all dead corpses.

In 2 Kings, we encounter a striking instance of angelic intervention in judgment. The angel of the Lord struck down 185,000 Assyrian soldiers in a single night.

Believer, the fourth revelation is that angels can execute swift and decisive judgment on God's behalf. This story reminds us of the sovereignty and power of God and the consequences of opposing Him. It also emphasizes the importance of aligning ourselves with God's purposes rather than standing against Him.

Revelation 8:6-7 - And the seven angels which had the seven trumpets prepared themselves to sound. The first angel sounded, and there followed hail and fire mingled with blood, and they were cast upon the earth: and the third part of trees was burnt up, and all green grass was burnt up.

In the book of Revelation, the seven angels with seven trumpets unleash a series of judgments upon the earth, including hail, fire, and blood.

Believer, the fifth revelation is that angels play a role in the judgment described in the book of Revelation. While these passages may depict future events, they remind us of the accountability of all creation before God. Let this truth spur you to live a life that honors God, recognizing that our actions have consequences both in this life and the one to come.

Matthew 13:41-43 - The Son of man shall send forth his angels, and they shall gather out of his kingdom all things that offend, and them which do iniquity; And shall cast them into a furnace of fire: there shall be wailing and gnashing of teeth. Then shall the righteous shine forth as the sun in the kingdom of their Father. Who hath ears to hear, let him hear.

In the parable of the wheat and tares, Jesus explains that the Son of Man will send His angels to gather out of His kingdom all things that offend and cast them into a furnace of fire. The righteous will shine forth in the kingdom of their Father.

Believer, the sixth revelation is that angels will be involved in the final separation of the righteous and the wicked. This parable underscores the importance of living a life that aligns with God's kingdom and righteousness. Let this truth motivate you to pursue a life of holiness and faithfulness to God's ways.

Matthew 16:27 - For the Son of man shall come in the glory of his Father with his angels; and then he shall reward every man according to his works.

Jesus Himself proclaims that He will come in the glory of His Father with His angels, and He will reward every person according to their works.

Believer, the seventh revelation is that angels will accompany Jesus in His return, and every individual will be rewarded based on their deeds. This truth underscores the accountability of our actions and the importance of living with an eternal perspective. Let it inspire you to live a life that seeks to honor God in all you do.

Hebrews 1:14 - Are they not all ministering spirits, sent forth to minister for them who shall be heirs of salvation?

The writer of Hebrews reminds us that angels are ministering spirits sent to minister to those who will inherit salvation.

Believer, the eighth revelation is that while angels are involved in executing judgment, they also serve and minister to God's children. Their role is not only one of justice but also of comfort and assistance to believers. Let this truth reassure you of God's care and protection in your life.

Now, as we contemplate angelic involvement in judgment, may you gain a deeper understanding of the divine order of justice and the believer's response to it. Angels serve as messengers of warning, agents of justice, and ministers of mercy. Let their role remind you of the importance of repentance, alignment with God's purposes, and living a life that honors Him. Ultimately, judgment is a reality, but it is accompanied by God's mercy and the hope of eternal reward for the righteous.

Chapter Thirteen

Exploring Divine Realms of Angels

In the preceding chapters of "Angels Unveiled," we've embarked on a remarkable journey through the angelic realm, uncovering their multifaceted roles in God's grand design. Yet, there's a vast and mysterious dimension to these heavenly beings that we have yet to explore—their existence within divine realms. In this chapter, we will delve into the depths of these divine realms of angels, drawing wisdom and inspiration from the timeless words of the King James Version of the Bible. These revelations are not mere intellectual pursuits; they are meant to be applied to the believer's personal life, inviting us to draw closer to God and embrace the spiritual realities that surround us.

Isaiah 6:1-3 - In the year that king Uzziah died I saw also the Lord sitting upon a throne, high and lifted up, and his train filled the temple. Above it stood the seraphims: each one had six wings; with twain he covered his face, and with twain he covered his feet, and with twain he did fly. And one cried unto another, and said, Holy, holy, holy, is the Lord of hosts: the whole earth is full of his glory.

The prophet Isaiah's vision provides a glimpse into the divine realm. He sees the Lord seated on a lofty throne, surrounded by seraphim with six wings, crying out, "Holy, holy, holy is the Lord of hosts."

Believer, the first revelation is that within the divine realms, angels engage in ceaseless worship of the Almighty. Their proclamation of God's holiness resounds throughout the heavenly places. Let this truth inspire you to cultivate a heart of worship, acknowledging the holiness and glory of God in every aspect of your life.

Daniel 7:10 - A fiery stream issued and came forth from before him: thousand thousands ministered unto him, and ten thousand times ten thousand stood before him: the judgment was set, and the books were opened.

In the book of Daniel, a vision reveals the heavenly court where thousands upon thousands minister to God, and the judgment is set with books opened.

Believer, the second revelation is that the heavenly realms are not only a place of worship but also the setting for divine judgment. Just as there is order and accountability in the heavenly court, there is a reflection of these principles in our earthly lives. Let this truth remind you of the importance of living a life of righteousness and accountability before God.

Revelation 4:2-3, 6b-8 - And immediately I was in the spirit: and, behold, a throne was set in heaven, and one sat on the throne. And he that sat was to look upon like a jasper and a sardine stone: and there was a rainbow round about the throne, in sight like unto an emerald...and round about the throne, were four beasts full of eyes before and behind. And the first beast was like a lion, and the second beast like a calf, and the third beast had a face as a man, and the fourth beast was like a flying eagle. And the four beasts had

each of them six wings about him; and they were full of eyes within: and they rest not day and night, saying, Holy, holy, holy, Lord God Almighty, which was, and is, and is to come.**

John's vision in the book of Revelation unveils the heavenly throne with four living creatures, each with six wings and full of eyes, continually declaring the holiness of the Lord God Almighty.

Believer, the third revelation is that the heavenly realms are filled with awe-inspiring creatures engaged in perpetual worship. These creatures remind us of the intricate and marvelous aspects of God's creation. Let this truth encourage you to appreciate the wonder and diversity of God's handiwork on Earth.

Revelation 5:11-12 - And I beheld, and I heard the voice of many angels round about the throne and the beasts and the elders: and the number of them was ten thousand times ten thousand, and thousands of thousands; Saying with a loud voice, Worthy is the Lamb that was slain to receive power, and riches, and wisdom, and strength, and honour, and glory, and blessing.

In the same heavenly vision, John witnesses the multitude of angels surrounding the throne, joining in a chorus of praise to the Lamb who was slain.

Believer, the fourth revelation is that the heavenly realms resound with the praises of countless angels, recognizing the worthiness of the Lamb who was slain. Their worship focuses on the redemptive work of Jesus Christ. Let this truth deepen your appreciation for the sacrificial love of Christ and inspire you to worship Him wholeheartedly.

Hebrews 12:22-23 - But ye are come unto mount Sion, and unto the city of the living God, the heavenly Jerusalem, and to an innumerable company of angels, To the general assembly and

church of the firstborn, which are written in heaven, and to God the Judge of all, and to the spirits of just men made perfect.

The writer of Hebrews reminds us that as believers, we have come to the heavenly Jerusalem and an innumerable company of angels, among other heavenly realities.

Believer, the fifth revelation is that as children of God, we are connected to the heavenly realms. We are part of a spiritual assembly that includes angels and the spirits of just men made perfect. This truth emphasizes our identity as citizens of heaven and calls us to live in a manner that reflects this heavenly citizenship.

Colossians 1:16 - For by him were all things created, that are in heaven, and that are in earth, visible and invisible, whether they be thrones, or dominions, or principalities, or powers: all things were created by him, and for him.

The apostle Paul declares that all things, whether in heaven or on earth, were created by Christ and for Him, including thrones, dominions, principalities, and powers.

Believer, the sixth revelation is that Christ is the Creator and Lord of all, including the heavenly realms. His sovereignty extends over every aspect of creation. Let this truth strengthen your trust in His lordship and authority in your life.

Ephesians 6:12 - For we wrestle not against flesh and blood, but against principalities, against powers, against the rulers of the darkness of this world, against spiritual wickedness in high places.

Paul's letter to the Ephesians reminds us that our battle is not against flesh and blood but against spiritual forces in high places.

Believer, the seventh revelation is that there is a spiritual battle taking place in the heavenly realms, involving principalities, powers, and spiritual wickedness. Our daily struggles are not merely physical but spiritual. Let this truth equip you to put on the armor of God and stand firm in spiritual warfare.

2 Corinthians 12:2-4 - I knew a man in Christ above fourteen years ago, (whether in the body, I cannot tell; or whether out of the body, I cannot tell: God knoweth;) such an one caught up to the third heaven. And I knew such a man, (whether in the body, or out of the body, I cannot tell: God knoweth;) How that he was caught up into paradise, and heard unspeakable words, which it is not lawful for a man to utter.

Paul shares an extraordinary experience of being caught up to the third heaven, where he heard unspeakable words.

Believer, the eighth revelation is that there are heavenly realms beyond our comprehension, where divine mysteries are unveiled. While we may not fully understand these realms, we can trust that God's wisdom and knowledge surpass our understanding. Let this truth encourage you to seek God's wisdom and revelation in your personal walk with Him.

May we explore the divine realms of angels, may you be filled with awe and wonder at the heavenly realities that surround us. The heavenly realms are places of worship, judgment, and intricate creation. As believers, we are connected to these realms through our identity in Christ. Remember that Christ is the Creator and Lord over all, including the spiritual battles that take place in the heavenly realms. Embrace your heavenly citizenship, put on the armor of God, and seek divine wisdom as you navigate the mysterious and awe-inspiring divine realms of angels.

Chapter Fourteen

―・◇・―

Maintaining a Balanced and Grounded Approach While Exploring Divine Realms

In our journey through "Angels Unveiled," we've ventured into the profound and mysterious world of angels, unraveling their roles, significance, and existence within divine realms. As we continue this exploration, we must recognize the importance of maintaining a balanced and grounded approach to these celestial realities. While the angelic realm is awe-inspiring, it can also be a source of fascination that leads us away from our foundation in Christ. In this chapter, we will delve into the scriptures, primarily from the King James Version of the Bible, to discern the wisdom needed to navigate this territory while remaining firmly grounded in our faith.

1 Corinthians 14:33 - For God is not the author of confusion, but of peace, as in all churches of the saints.

The apostle Paul reminds us that God is not the author of confusion but of peace. This truth underscores the need for clarity and order in our exploration of divine realms.

Believer, the first revelation is that our pursuit of spiritual truths, including the study of angels, should be marked by peace and order, not confusion or chaos. Let this truth guide your approach to exploring the heavenly realm, ensuring that it brings peace and edification to your faith.

1 Corinthians 2:9-10 - But as it is written, Eye hath not seen, nor ear heard, neither have entered into the heart of man, the things which God hath prepared for them that love him. But God hath revealed them unto us by his Spirit: for the Spirit searcheth all things, yea, the deep things of God.

Paul's letter to the Corinthians emphasizes that God has revealed the deep things of God to us through His Spirit.

Believer, the second revelation is that our understanding of divine realms and heavenly mysteries is made possible through the Holy Spirit's revelation. While we may not fully comprehend everything, God graciously reveals what we need to know. Let this truth encourage you to seek the guidance of the Holy Spirit in your exploration of spiritual truths.

Colossians 2:18-19 - Let no man beguile you of your reward in a voluntary humility and worshipping of angels, intruding into those things which he hath not seen, vainly puffed up by his fleshly mind, And not holding the Head, from which all the body by joints and bands having nourishment ministered, and knit together, increaseth with the increase of God.

In his letter to the Colossians, Paul warns against being beguiled by a false humility and worshipping of angels. He emphasizes the importance of holding onto Christ as the Head.

Believer, the third revelation is that our exploration of divine realms should never lead us to worship angels or become puffed up with spiritual pride. Instead, we must remain grounded in our relationship with Christ, recognizing Him as the Head of the body. Let this truth serve as a safeguard against any deviation from the true faith.

2 Corinthians 11:14 - And no marvel; for Satan himself is transformed into an angel of light.

Paul reminds the Corinthians that Satan can disguise himself as an angel of light.

Believer, the fourth revelation is that not all spiritual encounters are from God. Satan can deceive by appearing as an angel of light. Therefore, discernment is crucial in our exploration of divine realms. Seek the guidance of the Holy Spirit to discern the source and nature of any spiritual experience or encounter.

2 Timothy 3:16-17 - All scripture is given by inspiration of God, and is profitable for doctrine, for reproof, for correction, for instruction in righteousness: That the man of God may be perfect, throughly furnished unto all good works.

Paul's letter to Timothy underscores the significance of Scripture as a source of inspiration, doctrine, reproof, correction, and instruction in righteousness.

Believer, the fifth revelation is that the Word of God is our ultimate guide in exploring divine realms. It provides a solid foundation for our faith and offers correction and instruction. Let the Scriptures be your compass as you navigate the depths of spiritual truths.

Philippians 4:7 - And the peace of God, which passeth all understanding, shall keep your hearts and minds through Christ Jesus.

Paul assures the Philippians that the peace of God will guard their hearts and minds through Christ Jesus.

Believer, the sixth revelation is that the peace of God, which surpasses understanding, is a safeguard for your heart and mind. When exploring divine realms, if you feel anxious or unsettled, turn to God in prayer and seek His peace. Let His peace be the litmus test for the authenticity of your experiences.

1 John 4:1 - Beloved, believe not every spirit, but try the spirits whether they are of God: because many false prophets are gone out into the world.

John admonishes believers not to believe every spirit but to test them to determine if they are from God.

Believer, the seventh revelation is that discernment is a vital aspect of our faith. We are called to test the spirits and verify their origin. In the exploration of divine realms, this discernment is crucial to distinguish between authentic spiritual encounters and deceptive influences.

James 1:5 - If any of you lack wisdom, let him ask of God, that giveth to all men liberally, and upbraideth not; and it shall be given him.

James encourages us to seek wisdom from God, who generously gives it to all who ask.

Believer, the eighth revelation is that wisdom is readily available to those who seek it from God. In your journey through divine realms, do not hesitate to seek divine wisdom through prayer and study of the Word. It will provide you with the discernment and clarity needed to navigate these spiritual territories.

Psalm 19:14 - Let the words of my mouth, and the meditation of my heart, be acceptable in thy sight, O Lord, my strength, and my redeemer.

David's prayer in Psalm 19 expresses a desire for his words and meditations to be pleasing to the Lord.

Believer, the ninth revelation is that the meditations of our hearts and the words we speak should be pleasing to the Lord. In the midst of exploring divine realms, maintain a heart of humility and a spirit of reverence toward God. Let your thoughts and conversations align with the principles of faith and righteousness.

1 Thessalonians 5:21-22 - Prove all things; hold fast that which is good. Abstain from all appearance of evil.

Paul instructs the Thessalonians to test all things and hold fast to what is good while abstaining from all appearance of evil.

Believer, the tenth revelation is that we are called to discern what is good and abstain from anything that appears evil. In the exploration of divine realms, let discernment guide your choices and actions. Embrace what is aligned with God's truth and steer clear of anything that compromises your faith.

2 Timothy 1:7 - For God hath not given us the spirit of fear; but of power, and of love, and of a sound mind.

Paul reminds Timothy that God has given us a spirit of power, love, and a sound mind, not one of fear.

Believer, the eleventh revelation is that fear is not from God. As you journey through the exploration of divine realms, do not let fear hinder your faith. Instead, rely on the power, love, and sound mind that God has provided. Let these attributes empower you to navigate this spiritual terrain with confidence.

1 Peter 5:8 - Be sober, be vigilant; because your adversary the devil, as a roaring lion, walketh about, seeking whom he may devour.

Peter warns believers to be sober and vigilant, recognizing that the devil seeks to devour them.

Believer, the twelfth revelation is that spiritual vigilance is essential. While exploring divine realms, remain alert to the schemes of the enemy. Guard your heart and mind against deception, knowing that the devil seeks to undermine your faith. Stay rooted in prayer, the Word, and the fellowship of believers to withstand his attacks.

Now, as we maintain a balanced and grounded approach while exploring divine realms, may you be equipped with the wisdom, discernment, and peace needed to navigate these spiritual territories. Remember that God is not the author of confusion but of peace. Ground yourself in the Word of God, seek the guidance of the Holy Spirit, and remain vigilant against deception. Let your journey through divine realms be a source of growth and deeper intimacy with Christ, always holding onto Him as the Head of your faith.

Chapter Fifteen

———•·◇·•———

Connecting with Divine Guidance

In our journey through "Angels Unveiled," we've explored the wondrous world of angels, peeling back the layers of their divine roles and the mysteries of heavenly realms. Now, as we approach the culmination of our exploration, it's crucial to address a topic of immense significance—connecting with divine guidance. Angels, as messengers and servants of God, play a pivotal role in conveying His guidance to us. In this chapter, we will delve into the scriptures, primarily from the King James Version of the Bible, to uncover the profound truths about divine guidance and how we, as believers, can cultivate a deeper connection with it.

Psalm 32:8 - I will instruct thee and teach thee in the way which thou shalt go: I will guide thee with mine eye.

In this heartfelt psalm, David proclaims God's promise to instruct and teach us in the way we should go, guiding us with His watchful eye.

Believer, the first revelation is that divine guidance is a personal promise from God. He is intimately involved in our lives, offering to lead us in the right path. Let this truth instill confidence in you as you seek God's guidance in every aspect of your life.

Proverbs 3:5-6 - Trust in the Lord with all thine heart; and lean not unto thine own understanding. In all thy ways acknowledge him, and he shall direct thy paths.

Solomon's wisdom in Proverbs reminds us to trust in the Lord with all our hearts, lean not on our own understanding, and acknowledge Him in all our ways. In return, God promises to direct our paths.

Believer, the second revelation is that trust and acknowledgment of God are key to receiving divine guidance. Let go of self-reliance and instead place your complete trust in God. Acknowledge His sovereignty in every area of your life, and you will experience His guidance in profound ways.

Isaiah 30:21 - And thine ears shall hear a word behind thee, saying, This is the way, walk ye in it, when ye turn to the right hand, and when ye turn to the left.

Isaiah's prophecy assures us that God will speak to us, guiding us with His voice, even when we are uncertain which way to turn.

Believer, the third revelation is that divine guidance often comes as a still, small voice behind us, directing us in the way we should walk. Be attuned to God's voice, and heed His guidance, especially in moments of uncertainty.

John 14:26 - But the Comforter, which is the Holy Ghost, whom the Father will send in my name, he shall teach you all things, and bring all things to your remembrance, whatsoever I have said unto you.

Jesus promises the coming of the Holy Spirit, the Comforter, who will teach us all things and remind us of His teachings.

Believer, the fourth revelation is that the Holy Spirit is our divine guide and teacher. He brings to our remembrance the words and teachings of Jesus. Seek His guidance and rely on His wisdom as you navigate the complexities of life.

Acts 8:26-29 - And the angel of the Lord spake unto Philip, saying, Arise, and go toward the south unto the way that goeth down from Jerusalem unto Gaza, which is desert. And he arose and went: and, behold, a man of Ethiopia, an eunuch of great authority under Candace queen of the Ethiopians, who had the charge of all her treasure, and had come to Jerusalem for to worship, Was returning, and sitting in his chariot read Esaias the prophet. Then the Spirit said unto Philip, Go near, and join thyself to this chariot.

In this account from Acts, we witness the angel of the Lord and the Holy Spirit working in tandem to guide Philip to a divine encounter with the Ethiopian eunuch.

Believer, the fifth revelation is that angels and the Holy Spirit can work together to direct our paths and orchestrate divine encounters. Be open to their guidance, and trust that God's hand is leading you, just as it led Philip.

Acts 10:3-5 - He saw in a vision evidently about the ninth hour of the day an angel of God coming in to him, and saying unto him, Cornelius. And when he looked on him, he was afraid, and said, What is it, Lord? And he said unto him, Thy prayers and thine alms are come up for a memorial before God. And now send men to Joppa, and call for one Simon, whose surname is Peter.

In the case of Cornelius, an angel of God appears to him in a vision, instructing him to send for Peter. This angelic encounter plays a pivotal role in the unfolding of God's divine plan.

Believer, the sixth revelation is that angels can appear in visions to convey specific instructions. When you encounter such divine moments, like Cornelius did, be obedient to the guidance and direction provided.

Hebrews 1:14 - Are they not all ministering spirits, sent forth to minister for them who shall be heirs of salvation?

The writer of Hebrews reminds us that angels are ministering spirits sent to minister to those who will inherit salvation.

Believer, the seventh revelation is that angels are actively involved in ministering to us as heirs of salvation. They are God's messengers and servants, helping us along our journey of faith. Be open to their ministry and guidance as they fulfill their role in God's plan for your life.

James 1:5 - If any of you lack wisdom, let him ask of God, that giveth to all men liberally, and upbraideth not; and it shall be given him.

James encourages us to ask God for wisdom, and He will generously give it without reproach.

Believer, the eighth revelation is that wisdom is readily available to those who ask of God. As you seek divine guidance, ask for wisdom to discern His will and navigate life's decisions. Trust that God will generously provide the wisdom you need.

1 John 4:1 - Beloved, believe not every spirit, but try the spirits whether they are of God: because many false prophets are gone out into the world.

John advises us not to believe every spirit but to test them to determine if they are from God.

Believer, the ninth revelation is that discernment is essential when seeking divine guidance. Test the spirits to ensure their alignment with God's truth and character. Be cautious of false guidance that may lead you astray.

1 John 5:14 - And this is the confidence that we have in him, that, if we ask any thing according to his will, he heareth us:

John assures us that if we ask anything according to God's will, He hears us.

Believer, the tenth revelation is that when seeking divine guidance, align your requests with God's will. Trust that He hears your prayers and responds according to His perfect plan. Have confidence in His ability to guide you in His divine wisdom.

Revelation 3:20 - Behold, I stand at the door, and knock: if any man hear my voice, and open the door, I will come in to him, and will sup with him, and he with me.

In His message to the church in Laodicea, Jesus offers a profound invitation to hear His voice and open the door for fellowship.

Believer, the eleventh revelation is that Jesus desires intimate fellowship with us and actively seeks to communicate with us. Be attentive to His gentle knocking and open the door of your heart to receive His divine guidance and presence.

Revelation 22:8-9 - And I John saw these things, and heard them. And when I had heard and seen, I fell down to worship before the feet of the angel which shewed me these things. Then saith he unto me, See thou do it not: for I am thy fellowservant, and of thy

brethren the prophets, and of them which keep the sayings of this book: worship God.

In the closing of the book of Revelation, John witnesses glorious visions and falls down to worship the angel who showed them to him. The angel redirects his worship to God.

Believer, the twelfth revelation is that while angels play significant roles in divine guidance, they are not to be worshipped. Keep your worship focused solely on God, recognizing the angelic guidance as a means through which He communicates with you.

Revelation 22:17 - And the Spirit and the bride say, Come. And let him that heareth say, Come. And let him that is athirst come. And whosoever will, let him take the water of life freely.

In the final verse of Revelation, an invitation resounds for all who hear to come and partake of the water of life freely.

Believer, the thirteenth revelation is that God's invitation to divine guidance and eternal life is open to all who hear and respond. As you seek His guidance, remember that it is available freely to all who thirst for it.

Let us explore the profound topic of connecting with divine guidance, may you be filled with a renewed sense of God's presence and His desire to lead you. Divine guidance is not a distant concept but a tangible reality in the life of every believer. Trust in the promises of God's Word, seek the guidance of the Holy Spirit, and be attuned to the whispers of angelic messengers. With discernment and wisdom, you can navigate life's challenges, decisions, and uncertainties, confident that you are walking in the path that God has lovingly prepared for you.

Chapter Sixteen

The Art of Manifestation

In our journey through "Angels Unveiled," we have explored the marvelous realm of angels and the divine guidance they bring to our lives. Now, we come to a chapter that delves into a topic of profound significance—the art of manifestation. This chapter will guide us through the scriptures, primarily from the King James Version of the Bible, to uncover the spiritual principles of manifestation and how believers can apply these truths to experience God's blessings and fulfill His purpose in their lives.

Genesis 1:3 - And God said, Let there be light: and there was light.

Believer, the first revelation is that God's Word has the power to bring forth existence and change. Just as God spoke light into being, our words carry a unique creative power. When aligned with God's will and purpose, our declarations can manifest His blessings in our lives.

Proverbs 18:21 - Death and life are in the power of the tongue: and they that love it shall eat the fruit thereof.

The wisdom of Proverbs reminds us of the profound influence our words have. Life and death are in the power of the tongue, and we will reap the fruit of our speech.

Believer, the second revelation is that our words have a profound impact on our lives. Choose to speak life-affirming words that align with God's promises, and you will experience the fruit of God's blessings and provision.

Mark 11:23 - For verily I say unto you, That whosoever shall say unto this mountain, Be thou removed, and be thou cast into the sea; and shall not doubt in his heart, but shall believe that those things which he saith shall come to pass; he shall have whatsoever he saith.

In this teaching of Jesus, we discover the principle of speaking in faith. He assures us that if we believe without doubt and declare with faith, we will see the manifestation of our words.

Believer, the third revelation is that faith-filled declarations can move mountains and bring about the manifestation of God's promises in our lives. As you declare His truth with unwavering faith, you will witness the fulfillment of His purposes.

James 4:2 - Ye lust, and have not: ye kill, and desire to have, and cannot obtain: ye fight and war, yet ye have not, because ye ask not.

James highlights a significant aspect of manifestation—the power of asking. He points out that often, people do not receive because they fail to ask.

Believer, the fourth revelation is that asking is a vital part of the manifestation process. Approach God with your desires and needs in prayer, and you will open the door to His abundant provision and blessings.

Matthew 7:7 - Ask, and it shall be given you; seek, and ye shall find; knock, and it shall be opened unto you.

In Matthew's Gospel, Jesus encourages us to ask, seek, and knock, assuring us that we will receive, find, and have doors opened to us.

Believer, the fifth revelation is that persistence in asking, seeking, and knocking is a key to manifestation. Trust in God's faithfulness to answer your prayers and open doors in His perfect timing.

Psalm 37:4 - Delight thyself also in the Lord: and he shall give thee the desires of thine heart.

The psalmist David reveals a profound truth about manifestation—delighting in the Lord leads to the fulfillment of the desires of our hearts.

Believer, the sixth revelation is that when our delight is in the Lord, our desires align with His will. As a result, He grants the desires of our hearts in ways that bring joy and fulfillment.

John 15:7 - If ye abide in me, and my words abide in you, ye shall ask what ye will, and it shall be done unto you.

In His discourse with the disciples, Jesus imparts a powerful principle of manifestation. When we abide in Him and His words abide in us, our requests are granted.

Believer, the seventh revelation is that intimacy with Christ and a deep immersion in His Word pave the way for the manifestation of our requests. Align your desires with His Word, and see the transformation it brings to your life.

1 John 5:14-15 - And this is the confidence that we have in him, that, if we ask any thing according to his will, he heareth us: And if we know that he hear us, whatsoever we ask, we know that we have the petitions that we desired of him.

John assures us of the confidence we can have in God. When we ask in accordance with His will, we can be certain that He hears us and grants our requests.

Believer, the eighth revelation is that praying in alignment with God's will is a sure path to manifestation. Trust in His wisdom and sovereignty, and rest assured that your petitions will be granted in His perfect plan.

2 Corinthians 9:8 - And God is able to make all grace abound toward you; that ye, always having all sufficiency in all things, may abound to every good work.

Paul's letter to the Corinthians emphasizes God's abundant grace and sufficiency in all things. Believer, the ninth revelation is that God's grace is limitless and sufficient for every aspect of your life. As you trust in Him and seek His guidance, you will experience His abundant provision and be empowered for every good work.

Philippians 4:19 - But my God shall supply all your need according to his riches in glory by Christ Jesus.

Paul reassures the Philippian believers that God will supply all their needs according to His abundant riches.

Believer, the tenth revelation is that God is the ultimate source of provision in our lives. As you trust Him and manifest His promises through faith and declaration, you will experience His abundant supply in every area of your life.

Ephesians 3:20 - Now unto him that is able to do exceeding abundantly above all that we ask or think, according to the power that worketh in us,

Paul's letter to the Ephesians reminds us that God is able to do exceedingly abundantly above all we ask or think. The power of God works within us to bring about these manifestations.

Believer, the eleventh revelation is that God's power at work within us is the catalyst for extraordinary manifestations. As you yield to His power and believe in His limitless abilities, you will witness manifestations that surpass your expectations.

Romans 4:17 - (As it is written, I have made thee a father of many nations,) before him whom he believed, even God, who quickeneth the dead, and calleth those things which be not as though they were.

Paul references Abraham as an example of a faith-filled individual who believed in God's ability to call into existence things that did not yet exist.

Believer, the twelfth revelation is that the power of faith involves speaking things into existence that align with God's will. As you declare His promises with unwavering faith, you participate in the art of manifestation.

Hebrews 11:1 - Now faith is the substance of things hoped for, the evidence of things not seen.

The writer of Hebrews provides a profound definition of faith—it is the substance of things hoped for and the evidence of things not seen.

Believer, the thirteenth revelation is that faith is the substance that brings your hopes to reality and the evidence that precedes the manifestation of unseen things. Nurture your faith in God's promises, and you will witness the evidence of His faithfulness in your life.

Learning now, as we explore the art of manifestation, may you be inspired to align your words, desires, and prayers with God's will and purpose. Manifestation is not about pursuing selfish desires but about bringing God's blessings and purposes into your life and the lives of others. Trust in God's faithfulness, speak with faith, and persist in prayer. As you do so, you will experience the manifestation of His promises in ways that glorify Him and bring blessings to your life and those around you.

Conclusion

Reflecting on the Journey of Unveiling the Divine

As we come to the culmination of our journey through "Angels Unveiled," it's time to pause and reflect on the profound discoveries we've made together. We've ventured into the mysterious world of angels, explored divine realms, sought divine guidance, and delved into the art of manifestation. Now, in this chapter, we will take a moment to reflect on the journey of unveiling the divine and how these revelations can transform our personal lives. Let's turn to the scriptures, primarily from the King James Version of the Bible, to glean wisdom and inspiration for this reflective journey.

Psalm 119:105 - Thy word is a lamp unto my feet, and a light unto my path.

Believer, the first revelation we must hold dear is that the Word of God is our guiding light. Throughout our journey, we've relied on the scriptures to illuminate the path before us. As we reflect, let us remember that the Word of God will continue to be our source of guidance, clarity, and revelation in all seasons of life.

Psalm 34:8 - O taste and see that the Lord is good: blessed is the man that trusteth in him.

The psalmist invites us to taste and see the goodness of the Lord. This journey of unveiling the divine has allowed us to taste the goodness of God in the revelation of angels and divine realms.

Believer, the second revelation is that the journey of faith is a tasting and seeing of God's goodness. As we reflect on the revelations of angels and divine realms, let us trust in the Lord's goodness and blessings that flow from our faith in Him.

Proverbs 3:5-6 - Trust in the Lord with all thine heart; and lean not unto thine own understanding. In all thy ways acknowledge him, and he shall direct thy paths.

Solomon's wisdom in Proverbs reminds us of the importance of trust and acknowledging God in all our ways. This journey has reinforced the significance of trusting in the Lord with all our hearts and leaning not on our understanding.

Believer, the third revelation is that trust in God is the cornerstone of our journey. As we reflect, let us commit to trusting Him wholeheartedly and acknowledging His presence and guidance in every aspect of our lives.

Isaiah 30:21 - And thine ears shall hear a word behind thee, saying, This is the way, walk ye in it, when ye turn to the right hand, and when ye turn to the left.

The words of Isaiah remind us of God's guidance, which often comes as a gentle voice behind us, directing our steps. Throughout this journey, we've learned to listen for that guiding voice.

Believer, the fourth revelation is that God's guidance is always present, even when we are unsure which way to turn. As we reflect, let us continue to attune our ears to His voice and follow His direction, knowing that He leads us in the right path.

John 14:26 - But the Comforter, which is the Holy Ghost, whom the Father will send in my name, he shall teach you all things, and bring all things to your remembrance, whatsoever I have said unto you.

In the words of Jesus, we find the assurance that the Holy Spirit is our divine teacher and reminder of His teachings. This journey has reinforced the importance of relying on the Holy Spirit for guidance and revelation.

Believer, the fifth revelation is that the Holy Spirit is our constant companion, ready to teach us and bring Christ's teachings to our remembrance. As we reflect, let us continue to rely on the Holy Spirit's guidance in our daily lives and spiritual journey.

Acts 8:26-29 - And the angel of the Lord spake unto Philip, saying, Arise, and go toward the south unto the way that goeth down from Jerusalem unto Gaza, which is desert. And he arose and went: and, behold, a man of Ethiopia, an eunuch of great authority under Candace queen of the Ethiopians, who had the charge of all her treasure, and had come to Jerusalem for to worship, Was returning, and sitting in his chariot read Esaias the prophet. Then the Spirit said unto Philip, Go near, and join thyself to this chariot.

In the account of Philip and the Ethiopian eunuch, we witness the collaboration between angels and the Holy Spirit to orchestrate divine encounters. This journey has shown us the intricate workings of the heavenly realm in our lives.

Believer, the sixth revelation is that the heavenly realm is actively involved in orchestrating divine encounters and fulfilling God's purposes. As we reflect, let us remain open to the guidance of angels and the Holy Spirit, trusting that they are working together for our good.

Hebrews 1:14 - Are they not all ministering spirits, sent forth to minister for them who shall be heirs of salvation?

The writer of Hebrews reminds us of the ministry of angels, sent to minister to those who will inherit salvation. Our journey has unveiled the truth that angels are active participants in God's plan for our lives.

Believer, the seventh revelation is that angels are ministering spirits, serving us as heirs of salvation. As we reflect, let us appreciate their role in our lives and be open to their guidance and assistance in our spiritual journey.

James 4:2 - Ye lust, and have not: ye kill, and desire to have, and cannot obtain: ye fight and war, yet ye have not, because ye ask not.

James's words highlight the importance of asking in our journey of faith. This journey has reiterated the power of asking and seeking God's guidance and provision.

Believer, the eighth revelation is that asking is a crucial aspect of our journey. As we reflect, let us remember to approach God with our desires and needs, knowing that He is a loving Father who delights in providing for His children.

Romans 8:28 - And we know that all things work together for good to them that love God, to them who are the called according to his purpose.

Paul assures us that all things work together for good for those who love God and are called according to His purpose. Our journey has illuminated the truth that God's providence is at work in every circumstance of our lives.

Believer, the ninth revelation is that God's providence is always at work, shaping our journey for His divine purpose. As we reflect, let us trust in His sovereignty, knowing that even in challenging times, He is working all things for our good.

Philippians 4:19 - But my God shall supply all your need according to his riches in glory by Christ Jesus.

Paul's words to the Philippian believers remind us that God is the ultimate source of provision. Our journey has reinforced the truth that God is our faithful provider.

Believer, the tenth revelation is that God supplies all our needs according to His riches in glory. As we reflect, let us continue to rely on His provision, knowing that He is faithful to meet every need in our journey.

Revelation 21:5 - And he that sat upon the throne said, Behold, I make all things new. And he said unto me, Write: for these words are true and faithful.

In the revelation given to John, we are assured that God makes all things new. Our journey has shown us that God is in the business of transformation and renewal.

Believer, the eleventh revelation is that God's promise of making all things new is true and faithful. As we reflect, let us embrace the hope of transformation and renewal in our lives, trusting that God is at work in every season.

Revelation 22:17 - And the Spirit and the bride say, Come. And let him that heareth say, Come. And let him that is athirst come. And whosoever will, let him take the water of life freely.

In the closing words of Revelation, we hear the invitation resounding: **"Come". Our journey has unveiled the invitation to partake freely of the water of life.**

Believer, the twelfth revelation is that God's invitation to divine revelation and abundant life is open to all who hear and respond. As we reflect, let us continue to respond to His invitation, knowing that in Him, we find the source of life and revelation.

In conclusion, as we reflect on the journey of unveiling the divine, may you be filled with gratitude for the revelations and blessings that have unfolded. Remember that the journey continues, and God's faithfulness remains constant. Let the wisdom gleaned from our exploration of angels, divine realms, guidance, and manifestation be applied to your personal life as you walk in faith and trust, guided by the light of God's Word and the assurance of His providence.

It is my prayer that this book has been a blessing to you. May God continually draw you, closer to Himself, for His Glory. Amen.

www.ingramcontent.com/pod-product-compliance
Lightning Source LLC
LaVergne TN
LVHW051844080426
835512LV00018B/3065